Attention Seeking

a practical solution for the classroom

by

Nigel Mellor

Illustrations by Deborah Weymont

NORTH TYNESIDE COUNCIL

The book is dedicated to the families and schools of North Tyneside.

Lucky Duck Publishing Ltd. 1997
34 Wellington Park
Clifton
Bristol BS8 2UW
Phone or Fax 0117 973 2881 or 01454 776620
e-mail publishing@luckyduck.co.uk
website www.luckyduck.co.uk

ISBN 1 873942 76 1
Fourth printing February 2000

Acknowledgments.

I would like to extend my thanks to staff of the pupil support service and the many teachers and psychologists in North Tyneside who provided comments as this book developed.

Fleur Griffiths and Michelle Kirkpatrick provided some of the case study material.

The checklist on pages 27 to 28 is produced (in a slightly amended form) with permission of Addison Wesley Longman Ltd. The lengthy extracts about Elizabeth on pages 77 to 79 are reproduced with permission of B. Wade and M. Moore.

The survey of rewards on page 32 is from Burradon Primary school.

Particular thanks are due to George Robinson and Barbara Maines for their excellent editorial advice and to Dr. Sue Wressell, Val Besag and Chris Mearns for additional advice.

All names in case extracts have been changed.

The book has been produced with the support of North Tyneside Council. However, the views expressed do not necessarily reflect those of the Council.

First published May 1997
Reprinted September 1997, February 1999

Contents.

Overview

Part I : Practical Steps.

This section describes positive strategies for supporting the child who presents attention seeking behaviour in class. A procedure for identifying clear targets which could be included in Individual Education Plans is integral to the approach.

After a brief introduction, then observation and decision making exercises, the programme is laid out in three steps:

> 1. Initial stages.
> 2. The intervention.
> 3. Follow up plus trouble-shooting.

Case studies illustrate aspects of the approach as applied in a variety of settings.

Part II: The Context.

The theoretical background to the concept of attention seeking is the subject of the second half of the book.

Drawing on published case studies and relevant academic literature, this section provides additional ideas for overcoming problems which can arise in implementing programmes. It may also act as a starting point for those who wish to study the topic further.

Part I - Practical Steps.

Sounds familiar? The attention seeking child in class.

As an introduction to the topic of attention seeking in class, it can be very instructive first of all to call upon your own experience. One problem, however, in considering attention seeking behaviours is that almost anything could fall into this category - from nose picking to screaming. There is no simple checklist of "symptoms".

Here is an observation of Norman Young during one English lesson. He was constantly seeking attention in a variety of obvious and not so obvious ways. One pattern of his behaviour took some time to conceptualise; we called it "playing drums". Imagine a child sitting at his desk, jiggling about, moving all four limbs in rhythm and making a "tss, tss, tss" cymbal noise. (It is worth pointing out here that he was not "hyperactive". For some teachers he would sit and work quite happily - this issue is discussed later.)

Observation of Norman, age 12, during an English lesson in high school.

10.03	Crawls under T.V. towards cupboard. Flicks Darren's chair. Shouts at Luke.
10.04	Playing drums.
10.05	Flicking ruler.
10.06	Playing drums.
10.07	Playing drums.
10.08	Working.
10.09	Playing drums. Shouts out "Have you got to write the question?"
10.10	Giggling. Chatting. Playing drums.
10.11	Staring round. Chatting. Odd noises.
10.12	Chatting (continues for 8 minutes).
10.21	Chatting. Giggling. Knocks Julia's pencils off desk. Puts tongue out.
10.22	Working.
10.23	Knocks Julia's pencil case off again. Throws Andy's book. Coughs.
10.24	Shouting at Darren. Throws pencil case.
!0.25	Shouts out "Do you know who my uncle is?"
10.26	Scribbles on Lee's book. Makes loud "oo ah" noise. Pulls mouth to side with fingers.
10.27	Pulls mouth to side. Makes loud pig noises. Shouts to Luke.
10.28	Stares round. Plays drums.
10.29	Plays drums.
10.30	Stares round. Ruler in mouth. Knocks Julia's pencil case on floor. Plays drums. Sings. Whistles.

Attention seeking behaviour is immensely frustrating for the teacher:

> *He blocks me from all the other children. I've tried all sorts of ways of dealing with him and I get nowhere. He absorbs my energy, my attention. I give him so much and he gives nothing back. I start off feeling compassionate, I'd like to spend more time with him, then frustrated, then angry. He drains all the compassion from me. I feel like screaming. I feel like it's my fault. I'm just drained at the end of it.*
> **Art teacher discussing Michael Platt age 13 in high school.**

The secret in trying to understand such patterns is not to ask question "Why do they do it?" but to ask instead "What does the pupil appear to gain from behaving this way?" As McManus (1995) points out, asking a "Why?" question often leads to a pessimistic answer such as "It's the home background; what can I do about it?" If we consider instead the function that the behaviour serves for the pupil, we then discover clues to the practical steps we can take.

> *Kim seeks adult attention most of the time; this can either be by good behaviour, seeking praise for her work, or poor behaviour by making loud outbursts against others or leaping around the classroom.*
> **Teacher's comment on Kim Thomas age 10.**

Barry Sheen, age 7, gives a good example of the thousand and one ways children can act to gain attention in class.

Mrs. Lyons, Barry's teacher, described him as an intelligent boy but one who seemed unable or unwilling to follow instructions. If she said "walk" he would run; if she said "line up" he would continue writing or playing; in P.E. if she said "jump" he would skip.

Barry found it hard to co-operate and play with other children and had little idea of how to share. Generally, whoever he was working with or playing with would complain that Barry was cheating. If Barry was allowed to play in a group there was a constant stream of children complaining about him, coming to the teacher's desk, saying that he was snatching toys, pulling things apart etc. One of his favourite tricks was to bend other children's fingers and either kick, nip or punch them.

Mrs. Lyons mentioned several problems Barry displayed when working (it should be pointed out that the work was well within his ability). He clearly had heard instructions yet he regularly carried them out incorrectly. This rapidly drew the teacher over to him. Whenever Mrs. Lyons spoke to the class, Barry would question and challenge her. When she said, "Let's draw some people" Barry shouted out, "Why do we have to draw?" When his teacher was out in the yard preparing to ring the bell, Barry would immediately turn to run off. He would eventually saunter back to join the line.

When lining up in class he could not stand still. He would jump up and down, wave his arms about or run out of the line or change his position. When at the teacher's desk he would make a variety of noises: blow raspberries, click his tongue, break wind, burp, stamp his feet, thump the desk, anything to cause a disruption.

He seemed unable to keep his hands to himself, he was constantly fiddling with things, poking into other children's books and papers (as well as the teacher's), prising pictures off the wall, poking the tops of milk bottles, picking up other people's equipment and often throwing it across the room.

If he was sent out of the room for being naughty or allowed to go to the toilet, he would tear down displays, go through other children's coat pockets, throw the coats on the floor or mix them up on the pegs.

In P.E., Barry shouted and pushed all the way to the hall. He jumped under the safety rail instead of using the steps and pushed other children around. When told to stand apart from the other children Barry blew raspberries and pulled faces. When he was eventually sent out, he stood at the door pulling faces until he was told off again. On one occasion he held a sheet of paper in front of his face. When told by the head and various other teachers to lower it, Barry simply raised it further.

Mrs. Lyons said that he was a lovely child in the one-to-one setting and could be very endearing and affectionate and would also admit his mistakes. She also observed that "He just enjoys winding me up" and that he just seemed "to see how far he could go in disrupting the class". She added finally "I sometimes wonder if I am watching him too much". She was in fact quite close to realising herself that she had fallen into the trap that good, caring teachers fall in to - responding to the misbehaviour of a child who she was very concerned about. Her very strength became her weakness.

Attention seeking - the teacher's stress.

If you can identify similar problems then you most likely have had to deal with an attention seeking pupil. Children behaving in this manner, who require a great deal of attention, can cause their teachers great heartache, as Debbie's teacher recounts below :

Debbie Dawson, age 10, discussed in school with Ros Simpson (class teacher and special needs co-ordinator in Middle School).

Ros said, "She's a pain. She breathes for me. She's hanging onto my clothes, like a constant shadow." Ros then went on to say, "It's just attention seeking, pathetic really". However, she noted, "Your patience wears thin." She said that when giving instructions Debbie always asks questions and as soon as Ros has finished talking "I turn round and breathe and her hand is up,"

The teacher stated, "I couldn't say she's got a friend. Nobody wants to let her into the line. She winds everyone up."

As a result of this Debbie's table is separated from the other children otherwise, Ros said, "When working with them she would irritate them or complain that they were irritating her. They probably did but she probably instigated it".

Ros noted, "At break she is the only one the kids pick on (according to Debbie). She's always pestering for attention. There is nothing the matter or it's really trivial. One of these days she'll go to the office and there will be something wrong with her." (The implication was that Debbie was 'crying wolf'.) Ros felt there was a permanent miserable look on her face "she isn't nice to anyone and no-one is nice to her". In addition to this she is never in on time. She was late "every single morning and she only lives over the road".

Ros described her as irritating, "She's got me just about tearing my hair out; I can't think of one redeeming feature. I go home and I think I should be nice to her and I will try really hard with her".

She also said that Debbie tends to tell 'whoppers'. "She wouldn't know the truth if it jumped up and hit her. (When something happens) she always has a plausible story, she tells so many lies. She knows the difference between good and bad, she just gets it muddled up".

Ros had tried to be positive about her. "Debbie responds to praise but there are not a lot of occasions when this can be given. She can show a lovely little smile and is often 'dying to please you', however, I can't trust her to be a monitor".

Ros said, "Debbie had a nice relationship with Mrs. Nellis last year (but she was not really teaching her much then), it's when you've got her all the time. She irritates everyone, she is late to lessons, she is always late to first lesson and hasn't got her things. You could forgive her if it was out of the blue but it's every morning".

Ros said, "I veer between wanting to strangle her and give her a cuddle. She irritates me beyond words, then I get irritated because of that". She then also said, "she's not dim".

Part of the frustration is the teacher's feeling of helplessness. Normal procedures often appear to have opposite effects. The more the teacher tries, the worse the problem becomes. Miss Vernon, for instance, was quite upset about Martin Cummings age 8. On his own he was an angelic blond blue-eyed boy, butter wouldn't melt in his mouth. She said,

> *Punishments don't seem to bother him, there's nothing you can do to reach him. He wants my reaction, he very much wants to see what I'll do to him next. When I'm busy, that's when he starts. There's no relief - he is very able so I can't put him with the special needs children. I'm making a rod for my own back; he does things you can't ignore.*

One of the most distressing features of attention seeking can be the "punishment paradox" where punishment does not suppress misbehaviour but acts instead as a reinforcement (this issue is discussed again on page 39).

Activity - what do they gain from behaving this way?

- Think back to those children you have found most irritating and annoying to teach over the years, or ask colleagues for their recollections.

- Make a brief note of what these children actually did which caused the annoyance (and try to recall your feelings at the time).

- Try to answer the question "What did they gain from behaving this way?"

Attention seeking - a round up.

Norman, Michael, Barry and Debbie all demand a great deal of attention. The best guide to identifying such cases is simply your own feelings of irritation or annoyance. Balson (1982) explores other emotions teachers may commonly experience such as feeling challenged, hurt or helpless. These, he argues, characterise reactions to pupils seeking not attention but power, revenge or withdrawal respectively.

The children can themselves be quite insightful about the situation. Here is Lucy Nugent age 13 in high school discussing herself and her younger siblings in a step-family:

> *I get the most money, Mark and Ben get the most attention. Mum is always helping them. Ben is his [step father's] son, he gets more attention than me.*

Neil Robson age 12, discussing short stories about children, commented about one example:

> *He really wanted attention. If the teacher's always busy you do things so she notices you as well.*

Debbie, who we discussed above, describing one child's behaviour in a short story, said,

> *She might have wanted attention, people to pet her up and everything - because people at home were not looking after her and there was a new baby.*

The attention seeking child is seen by many teachers as the most common problem in school (Balson 1982). In many texts on behaviour problems the idea of attention seeking appears not at all or at best, fleetingly. However, the Elton committee reported that it was not getting "beaten up" which concerned most teachers most of the time, but gradually getting " ground down" by constant annoyances. Attention seeking interactions are a main cause of stress experienced by teachers.

> *In isolation many of the examples [of misbehaviour].... appear to be relatively trivial ... [but such] problems led to a sense of being slowly worn down*
>
> **D.E.S. 1989 p.254.**

Attention seeking - towards a definition.

As a working definition, attention seeking will be taken in this book to refer to those behaviours which, through their very irritating nature, bring a child to the attention of a number of adults in a persistent manner over a lengthy period of time, causing great concern. We would exclude, for instance, the sudden reaction of a child to an upset at home lasting for a few days or weeks. In addition, the pattern should appear in more than one setting (e.g. with several teachers or with teacher and parents/carers).

Unfortunately, the term attention seeking has a pejorative ring to it with an implication of conscious motivation by the child. Our experience shows that this style is one that the child has adopted over a period of time. The interactions seem to have become more of a habit than a deliberate strategy, although at times a clear intent may be apparent. In any case, the need for change lies with the adults. We cannot rely on counselling the child to achieve a solution.

The phrase also conceals the circular nature of the affair, that the adult and child are both locked in an interaction. The child is evidently seeking attention but a more neutral terminology such as **attention needing** might be recommended.

Taking account of the very unusual behaviours children sometimes exhibit when trapped into an attention seeking cycle it is often tempting to look for a "medical" cause. This is a topic we shall explore later. Often a confused mixture of "explanations" is around. These are sometimes implied rather than stated, and may be mutually contradictory, as we grasp for understanding. Nicholas Noble's mum, for instance, mused,

> "He can be good but has 'radgie' days. I wonder if it was the food. With his weight and glasses, they're skitting him all the time. Last year his grandma died. He just likes being the centre of attention. Can't we hypnotise him?"

For now, the words of one consultant paediatrician about a very attention seeking five year old seem appropriate:

> "It is my impression that his behavioural difficulties are likely to be of an attention seeking nature rather than being due to seizures or other organic brain defect".

The next section considers positive steps to deal with this situation.

Warning.

Things can get worse before they get better!

Any intervention such as this, which aims to prevent children gaining attention in ways which have become a habit, runs a risk. In the early stages, the child may notice first a reduction in attention given.

Although a key element in the strategy is praise, as adults we often find it difficult to make quite the impact when praising acceptable behaviour that we make when reprimanding. In addition, as another key element is ignoring, the child may feel overall that less attention is available. He or she is thus likely to misbehave even more to regain this lost attention, a tactic which has worked in the past.

Patience in persisting with the programme will, however, pay off eventually. So, don't lose heart if things appear to deteriorate for a while - that means the approach is working! The pupil has already responded to a difference in your behaviour.

Starting the programme
- looking at your own behaviour in class.

Dealing with attention seeking is tremendously challenging and it can be very painful to examine your own reactions in class. However, this is an important starting point.

One vital aspect of the programme concerns those periods when the pupil displays acceptable behaviour (these may be few and far between!). In the table below we can see how the teacher's time is so taken up dealing with the irritations that the short period of productive work is easily overlooked.

Time	Susie	Teacher
10.24	Looking at wall	"Can you make a start?"
	"Need a pencil"	
	"Need a calculator Sir"	"You know where they are"
	"Are they in the drawer?"	
10.25	Pokes Carol	"If you two can't sit together"
	Pats Carol on back and talks	"One and only one warning you
10.26	Idling	two"
10.27	Idling	
10.28	On task working quietly	NO RESPONSE
10.29	On task working quietly	NO RESPONSE
10.30	Chews sweets very openly	"If you're going to eat sweets, keep your mouth closed"
10.31	Idling	
10.32	Pokes Carol with book and says in bad-tempered voice,	
	"Pass me that pencil"	
	"Is there a ruler in here Sir?"	
	"Can I go to the canteen?"	"Susie!"
10.33	Pokes Carol and talks	"Listen, stop the chatting!"
	"But I'm doing my work"	
10.34	Idling	
10.35	Idling	
10.36	Pokes Carol	"Just do your work Susie"
	"I've dropped my money"	
10.37	Gets eraser, rubs on bench, argues with Carol.	"Can you just stop your messing about you two? Susie, move across"
10.38	"Why are you always picking on me?"	"Look, settle down"

Activity - observing your own interactions with an attention seeking child.

♦ Arrange for a trusted colleague to observe you in your class. If this is not possible, select a time when you will feel under least pressure and make a simple record of your own behaviour. Remember that objective observation is extremely difficult :

Too often we see only what we want or expect to see rather than what has actually taken place.

Montgomery 1989 p.83.

♦ Focus the observation on a child you can identify as attention seeking.

♦ Try to obtain a record of when you interact with the pupil and the reasons for doing so using the observation schedule below.

♦ Examine this record to discover when your interactions with the pupil occur. Are they most frequent when he or she is productively engaged or are you dragged into interacting as a result of his or her inappropriate behaviours?

Observation Schedule.

Make a tick in one or other column each time you react in some way to the pupil. Your response may be either verbal or non-verbal such as simply looking in the pupil's direction or frowning. Children are very adept at picking up these non-verbal signs and they can provide a much needed source of attention, together with a host of other unintended consequences such as providing a brief entertainment and giving the child a feeling of power.

Teacher reacted when pupil was "on task"	Teacher reacted when pupil was "off task" or otherwise behaving inappropriately

If most of your ticks appear in the second column then, quite unintentionally, you may be encouraging the pupil to maintain the very behaviours you want to eliminate. Teacher attention of any kind, positive or negative, is a very powerful pay-off for the child who is hungry for attention.

Before beginning a programme to deal with this, however, it is necessary to clear up some preliminaries. These are outlined in the next section.

A programme for dealing with attention seeking - some preliminaries.

These are some questions to try to answer before starting to intervene. You may have to read on first to get a feel for the whole programme then come back to this section later in order to answer some of the queries. There may be more than one pupil giving concern. If this is your first attempt at such an approach it could be an advantage if you do not begin with the most difficult case. It may be wise to gain confidence by applying the techniques first to a child with whom you are more likely to succeed.

1. Is this the best time to start?

It may not be a good idea to start at the end of a term when everyone is tired or when special activities are due to happen. Is this the best time for you? There is no requirement to rush into the programme. There are many tasks to carry out before beginning any intervention, such as making baseline observations, choosing rewards, or arranging discussions with parents and special needs co-ordinator.

Do you have the physical and emotional resources to carry through the programme right now? If not, when would be the best time to start?

Might it be better to wait, if, for instance, a new school discipline approach or some other initiative is being planned?

2. Can you gain parents' support?

Discuss this with your special needs co-ordinator, who may want to refer to the psychologist for your school in the most serious cases. You should, however, be able to involve parents quite readily (e.g. by arranging for extra rewards at home for improvements at school or by running a positive home-school diary).

3. Can you justify this intervention?

Could you help the child in another way? Discussions with your special needs co-ordinator may reveal areas which have been overlooked, and which, if tackled, could avoid the need for this intervention (see below).

This programme asks the teacher to take a special approach to the pupil who is misbehaving. Make sure you feel comfortable with all aspects of the programme before starting (especially the sections on rewarding and ignoring).

4. Is the pupil actually seeking attention? Is your analysis accurate?

Try to clarify whether there are other difficulties which might call for different forms of support. Discuss these other aspects with your special needs co-ordinator. This book does not cover the whole range of school based troubles which might occur.

The distinctions outlined below are not research-based but arise from experience. They are offered as rough "rules of thumb" to help guide the class teacher whose access to outside professional advice may be limited. They must be used with caution and, wherever possible, backed up with other opinion. The teacher should be aware that many of these conditions can appear in various combinations. They may all, in addition, respond well to the kind of individual support and careful management found to be effective with attention seeking children.

One useful principle is that any instance of unusual behaviour which could be attention seeking should be part of a long standing pattern to acquire the designation "attention seeking" correctly. Thus stealing, lying, truancy etc. which are not accompanied by other irritating, annoying behaviours in class would probably not be best handled as part of an attention seeking repertoire. Again, great caution should be exercised in making these subtle differentiations.

A. Attention deficit hyperactivity disorder, ADHD.

Attention seeking is easily confused with many other difficulties in school. A similar sounding label is "attention deficit hyperactivity disorder". Broadly speaking this label refers to children with problems of **paying attention** (to their work) not problems of **demanding attention** (from their teachers), together with associated difficulties of being overactive and impulsive. These are children who cannot concentrate and who may be constantly restless. For further information see Taylor 1994, Green and Chee 1995, O'Brien 1996 or BPS 1995.

As a very rough way of distinguishing the two we can focus on the "hyperactivity" aspects of ADHD and attention seeking. The child who displays a great deal of activity in class as a way of obtaining attention will almost certainly be happy to settle to work quite calmly with the teacher 1:1. If the child continues to fidget and move all the time and you suspect ADHD discuss this with your special needs co-ordinator and school medical officer. Management techniques (at home and school) and medication may both be necessary for ADHD as the following case illustrates:

> *Simon Jenkins had difficulties in first school which his mother and school agreed to tackle quite successfully as attention seeking. When problems recurred in middle school Mrs. Jenkins took a medical route. Simon was diagnosed as having ADHD and prescribed medication. His concentration improved greatly and his behaviour settled for a while then deteriorated. The underlying management issue remained. At a recent home visit his grandmother commented, "She [Simon's mother] can't get him to do anything. They argue all the time - like brother and sister".*

Mrs. Jenkins reported at a recent review that she had joined a parents' group at the hospital and was relieved to find she was not alone in having problems. She agreed she still needed to change her approach because in the house "He likes to be boss". His teacher also noted that, although the drugs helped, Simon required clear guidelines; he was not happy about them, however.

B. Bullying.

The school should have a policy on dealing with bullying if it is occurring. (Robinson and Maines, 1994.) This is a very serious issue and should be tackled with great care. It is obviously important that genuine cases of bullying are identified. However, as discussed earlier, almost any behaviour could be designed to attract attention. Being involved in bullying, as bully or victim, can be part of this pattern. Besag (1989) mentions the category of "false victims" :

> *... children who complain unnecessarily about others in the group. It is usually attention-seeking behaviour (p.14).*

Such children may need teacher help in a number of ways, but their behaviour may be part of an attention seeking interplay. As another very rough guide, in some instances, attention seeking children may revel in their victim role to extract maximum attention. Victims of serious bullying may on the other hand feel shame and fear and try to hide their experiences.

C. Learning difficulties.

Boredom, fear of failure and alienation also need to be seen as potential causes of displacement activities such as attention seeking (Montgomery 1989 p.10).

> *All too often, children try to hide their feeling of academic inadequacy by "fooling around" or using some form of displacement activity such as "losing books ... continuously breaking and sharpening pencils... ignoring instructions and talking to others" (ibid p.13).*

It is essential to establish that the pupil can cope with the curriculum on offer in the mainstream school and to rule out learning difficulties as a causal factor in attention seeking behaviours. Karl age 8 years, for example, had excellent practical skills but very poor verbal skills. His behaviour problems arose from his learning difficulties, as his psychologist's report makes clear. It would be inappropriate to see his main trouble as attention seeking:

> *Karl is self-conscious enough to be keen to avoid failure in front of his classmates. So he goes quiet and withdraws into time-wasting activities, or diverts attention from work by over-excited, rather immature, clowning behaviour. In the place of words, he has at times physically overpowered others in his attempts to be friendly.*

Simply having learning difficulties does not necessarily lead to attention seeking. Most children in special school settings do not display attention seeking behaviour. Some do, however, and strategies for support in special schools and units parallel those in mainstream, with due allowance for the individual needs of the pupil in question. Dave Norris below is a good illustration.

> *Dave was a cheerful, chatty lad age 13. However, assessment showed that his understanding of language was only at the 1st centile. He had hydrocephalus and a shunt had been inserted. Dave attended a school for children with physical impairments. The school had become increasingly concerned about him. As the deputy head teacher commented, "His name is never out of the head's report book".*

> *Dave could be extremely irritating and annoying throughout the day both in and out of class. Some of the items were minor. For instance, on one occasion he claimed to have lost his dinner money but the school found he had hidden it. A few weeks previously he came into school with his trousers on the wrong way round. Many incidents were more serious, such as fighting, swearing, running into the girls' toilets and dropping his trousers, hitting the more vulnerable children or 'disappearing' at breaks. The cumulative effect was very wearing. His teacher noted, "Dave likes being kept in at break, it's no deterrent - it's a punishment to go out". The deputy commented, "He's happy as Larry doing jobs such as sharpening pencils for the five year olds".*

In one school for children with severe learning difficulties, Dan Usher age 14, had a slightly different pattern of behaviour for each of his three settings: home, classroom and respite care. The common thread, however, was that they all brought attention. This theme of the continuity behind apparently very different behaviours is explored later.

D. Attendance problems.
It is important to recognise attention seeking as a possible factor in non-attendance. Blagg (1987) for instance cites the case of Elvie, age 13 who had been refusing school for sixteen weeks. She was *"jealous of the attention the younger child received from both the grandparents and the mother"* (p 176). Whatever the original trigger for her non-attendance *"she derived much pleasure from being the centre of attention in the family"* as a result of her absences (ibid p.178). Parents were eventually persuaded to take a firm line with her and *"special treats, attention and fuss reserved ... for the evenings ... after she managed to attend school"* (ibid p.177).

Obviously here, detailed discussion with parents is generally the key to uncovering such a background. The class teacher will have to call on outside agencies for support.

E. Stealing.

> *Young children's stealing is often an indication of their need for affection and esteem (Montgomery 1989 p.53).*

As a result of the arrival of a new baby or step-parent, for instance,

> *"...'comforting' offences [such as stealing] become common or bed wetting suddenly restarts " (ibid p.53).*

The case study of Elizabeth, described later, illustrates stealing as part of attention seeking for a child jealous of her twin. As a very rough guide, the attention seeking child may ensure that the stealing (often of minor items) and the culprit are easily discovered. The gain for the child may not be the objects but the fuss surrounding their discovery. As one teacher commented about Terry Downs age 10 in middle school: *"The shoplifting is secondary. He wants a reaction. He wants us to show care and concern".*

If other reasons for stealing seem to predominate (Montgomery 1989, for instance, identifies "marauding", "proving" and "secondary" offences) alternative, long term approaches may be more relevant (see for example Dawson 1985).

F. Social skills deficits.
Some children have difficulties in interacting with others and may display squabbling, poor friendship skills and poor communication skills.

> *... many pupils with behaviour problems have poor social skills. When they engage in socially disapproved behaviour they have insufficient social skills to negotiate themselves out of the trouble this creates.*

Montgomery 1989 p.5.

The attention seeking pupil may show a rather different pattern, however. As a rough guide (often from parents' report) the pupil may be found to relate perfectly well to much younger or much older children who do not provide immediate competition. Problems are usually focused on the child's own age group. The attention seeking child may, in addition, communicate excellently with adults when no other children are around to absorb the teacher's attention (such as when being kept in a break time). Social skills deficits which occur in all settings require more specialised programmes which the special needs co-ordinator may be able give advice on (see for instance Dawson 1985).

Activity - clarifying the full range of support needed.

Bearing in mind that many "problems" may be attention seeking in disguise and that the reverse may also be true - what is seen as attention seeking may hide a real need in some other area - try to complete the following chart:

Identified "problem"	Possible approaches and who can advise	Could this be part of an attention seeking pattern?

Guidelines for developing a programme.

♦ Given the pressure of classroom life, a successful programme has to be simple. Keep it well within the limits of what you think you can maintain.

♦ Your special needs co-ordinator may be able to help, for example in identifying the positive behaviours of a very irritating child.

♦ The approach suggested does not encourage you to give **more time** to the attention seeking pupil. It invites you to re-direct your time so that you give the pupil the **same amount** of time, but **when you decide**, not when the child demands it. The long term aim is to reduce the amount of time you spend dealing with inappropriate behaviour.

♦ The guidelines suggest stages that will help you devise strategies for dealing with attention seeking behaviour. A particular trick in the initial stages is to use the negative behaviours to generate ideas for positive behaviours by "turning them inside out" (see page 28).

These guidelines break down into three sections:

1. **Initial stages.**
2. **The intervention.**
3. **The follow up.**

1. Initial Stages.

Activity - focusing on existing positive behaviours.

Although your main concern will be with the irritating behaviours the pupil produces, and these are tackled below, the most successful approaches utilise the full range of the child's activities. Such programmes build on existing positive behaviours as well as addressing the less acceptable aspects. It is often easy to lose sight of the positive aspects of attention seeking children.

To develop this strategy, you may wish complete the following table to highlight existing positive behaviours you would like to encourage. They will be included in the programme later and can form part of an I.E.P.

Positive behaviours	
Positive behaviours the pupil already displays regularly.	Positive behaviours which appear sometimes but which you wish to see more often
e.g. always comes on time e.g. always has equipment	e.g. can produce very neat work e.g. can work well in a group on project work

Activity - focusing on negative behaviours.

The main concern of the programme is, of course, those irritating, negative or unacceptable behaviours you encounter in your classroom. We can best tackle these in two steps :

- ◆ **First step:**   identifying the "negative" behaviours.
- ◆ **Second step:** turning these negative behaviours into positives to target in your programme.

First step: identifying the "negative" behaviours.

- ◆ The checklist below is provided to help this process. The list is meant to cover all age ranges. Just omit those items which seem inappropriate and add any others you wish, to tailor your observations more accurately.

- ◆ Using this bank of items, draw up your own list of "negative" behaviours that the pupil displays. Try to be as objective as possible. Avoid vague fuzzies such as "disruptive"; use concrete descriptions such as "jumps on desk" instead.

- ◆ Keep a count of how often these negative behaviours occur. You may need to arrange separate observation sessions to do this. If that is not possible, you will have to rely on your memory at the end of the lesson and make a rough estimate.

Behaviour Checklist	Date	Name of pupil

A. Relating to children

1 Carries on distracting conversation
    with another pupil
2 Shouts to another pupil
3 Verbally abuses another pupil
4 Spits at another pupil
5 Mimics another pupil
6 Passes food/drink to another pupil
7 Hits another pupil
8 Pokes another pupil
9 Kicks another pupil
10 Pushes another pupil
11 Jumps onto another pupil
12 Trips another pupil
13 Bites another pupil
14 Scratches another pupil
15 "Strangles" another pupil
16 Indirectly hurts another pupil
    e.g. drawing pin on chair
17 Verbally threatens another pupil
18 Physically threatens another pupil
    Other:

C. Sitting and moving

1 Turns round in seat (inappropriately)
2 Rocks in chair
3 Sits out of position in seat
4 Fidgets / lolls about
5 Shuffles chair
6 Stands up (inappropriately)
7 Changes seat (inappropriately)
8 Moves from seat (inappropriately)
9 Walks about class (inappropriately)
10 Runs about class
11 Leaves classroom
12 Climbs on furniture
13 Lies on floor
14 Crawls on floor
    Other:

B. Relating to teacher and work

1 Arrives late
2 Enters room noisily
3 Leaves coat on
4 Fails to bring equipment/book
5 Fails to do homework
6 Fails to do punishment work/attend
    detention
7 Carries on distracting conversation
    with teacher
8 Shouts at teacher
9 Argues with teacher
10 Silently fails to follow teacher's
    instructions
11 Mimics teacher
12 Verbally abuses teacher directly/
    under breath
13 Clings to teacher
14 Indirectly hurts teacher, e.g.
    practical joke
15 Hits teacher
16 Verbally threatens teacher
17 Physically threatens teacher
18 Does very little work
19 Sits and plays
20 Packs away early
21 Fails to leave classroom
22 Eats/drinks
    Other:

D. Communication (general)

1 Cries
2 Laughs/giggles inappropriately
3 Makes noises
4 Whistles
5 Sings
6 Tells lies
7 Pulls funny faces
8 Makes inappropriate gestures
9 Talks to self
10 Swears to self or others
11 Shouts across class
    Other:

E. Equipment	F. Other behaviours

1 Moves furniture
2 Throws pellets/paper
3 Throws equipment/books
4 Throws furniture
5 Bangs furniture
6 Stamps feet
7 Taps hands on furniture
8 Taps pencil / ruler etc.
9 Moves or takes other's equipment
10 Damages own equipment or work
11 Damages other's equipment or work
   Other:
	1 Writes on furniture / equipment
	2 Writes on wall
	3 Spits on floor
	4 Disarranges clothes
	5 Hurts self / pretends to
	6 Pretends to be ill
	7 Pretends to need the toilet
	8 Plays with or strikes matches
	   Other:

Adapted from Grunsell (1985).

Second step: turning these negative behaviours into positives to target in your programme.

Consider each of the negative behaviours you identified in the above checklist. Try to turn each one of these "inside out" and write the positive behaviour you would like to see in its place and complete the following table. These new items can also be included in an I.E.P.

Activity - turning behaviours "inside out".

Negative behaviours you have observed	Positive behaviours you want
e.g. Shouts out e.g. Walks round class e.g. Hits Jim e.g. Pokes Gemma with pencil	Talks quietly Stays on seat Sits nicely next to Jim Writes with pencil

2. The Intervention.

You are now in a position to implement the programme. In a nutshell it suggests you ignore where you can, give low key punishments where you can't and dole out bags of praise. But that's where the problems begin. The most obvious, apparently simple techniques, those we use every day with little thought, are those which require the utmost care when dealing with an attention seeking child. Five areas should be carefully considered:

    A.   **Target behaviours.**
    B.   **Recording.**
    C.   **Rewards.**
    D.   **Planned ignoring.**
    E.   **Punishment.**

A. Target behaviours.

The behaviours to focus on can include:

◆ Those positive aspects you originally identified (which you simply wish to encourage).

◆ Those new positive behaviours you generated by turning the negatives "inside out".

◆ Where appropriate, negotiate the target behaviours with the pupil.

◆ When you see these positive behaviours, try to find time to go over to the pupil for a few seconds and praise him or her or give some other small reward.

◆ Remember, the aim of the approach is not to give the pupil more of your time. The aim is to try to give the same amount you give now, but when you decide i.e. when the pupil is behaving the way you want. This returns control to you, the teacher.

◆ Record these positive behaviours on a simple chart. There are several varieties depending on the age/interests of the pupil and the time you have available to complete them. Some examples are provided on pages 60 - 70. Select one you feel will be most useful, given the time pressures you have. Some children will enjoy completing the charts themselves.

♦ As well as using your praise and positive attention as rewards, try to make sure other reinforcements are available (see page 32 - 34).

♦ You may find it helpful to change the rewards if their impact drops off over time.

B. Recording.

There are many ways to record behaviour. For younger children it is important that any chart used is attractive and appeals to the particular pupil. Some teachers have used photo copied line drawings of the child's favourite cartoon character and marked these off in sections so that each section can be coloured in turn as the desired behaviours mount up. For older pupils a simple tick on a list will often suffice.

The charts can be very individual. One child, for instance, who was crazy about cars, had a chart in the form of a race track with numbered squares to travel round towards his goal. Another child coloured in sections of a T-shirt. One child had a page full of computers to colour in to earn time on the computer. In one classroom the teacher recorded a child's behaviours by dropping marbles in a jar. In this case the marbles not only acted as a record, they provided an immediate reward (the child loved the "click"). Hanging extra pieces onto a mobile for each positive behaviour can be quite effective both as a reward and a record; in one class where the children had been reading about native Americans, the teacher used feathers in a headband to record and reward one pupil. The possibilities are limited only by our imagination. Use the examples provided or design your own.

C. Rewards.

♦ For most children praise and a positive letter sent home are the two most powerful rewards available. Many children enjoy certificates and points earned in class. Celebration also has a powerful impact (Robinson and Maines 1995).

♦ Reinforcements must be readily and quickly available. Expecting the attention seeking child to work towards rewards at the end of the week or even the end of the day will probably be asking too much.

♦ Research indicates that we happily reward good work. We are generally less ready to reward good behaviour (Schwieso and Hastings 1987).

♦ It is important to be tactful with teenagers. Overt, lavish praise can be embarrassing. Note also that the child who is very self critical may react against praise. He "knows" his work is no good - your praise simply makes him annoyed. He may destroy his work in response (Balson 1982).

♦ Some children may cope well with self monitoring: keeping a diary of 'Good Things' or updating a list of their positive assets or completing a success book on a regular basis (Docking 1993).

♦ It is also worth considering the idea of encouragement for trying, rather than praise for succeeding:

Teachers who accept and value students as they are now, who convey faith in their ability to learn and develop, and who recognize and acknowledge genuine effort or improvement will create a learning environment ... based on mutual trust and respect - the essential ingredients for encouragement

(Balson 1982 p. 99).

♦ Remember "Grandma's Rule" - "first you work, then you play" (Herbert 1981 p.56) i.e. self-chosen activities can be used as reinforcements after a task has been accomplished. Thus, make it clear that the routine is, for example, ten minutes quiet reading followed by five minutes on the computer.

♦ Some additional ideas for rewards are listed later, collected under the headings Social, Activities, Concrete and Internal. They may or may not be suitable for the pupil you are concerned about. The important question to ask always is, "is this 'reward' actually rewarding for this pupil?"

♦ Involve parents in this as far as possible. For example, get their agreement to back up a positive home-school report which focuses simply on "good behaviour". Encourage them to provide additional reinforcement at home. This does not have to be expensive: extra praise; trips to the park; staying up late; friends to sleep over; mum getting in the swimming pool; child's choice for the Saturday night take-away and video etc.

♦ Be alert to the danger of becoming routine and stale and losing enthusiasm. The pupil will notice! Over a long period, however, rewards can eventually be tapered off or given more randomly, to maintain success.

♦ One primary school carried out a reward survey. You may want to try repeating this in your class to get further ideas on what may motivate the child you are concerned about. The children in the survey were asked to decide which rewards they thought would be fair for various things which could happen in school. They could list anything which did not cost the school money. Below are the results:

Things which could happen.	Most popular reward
Completing all the work on time	Sticker
Finishing a piece of work they found hard	Certificate
Trying to do all their work in the lesson without asking the teacher to help	Letter home
Doing a job in the classroom for the teacher	Smile
Remembering to bring their reading book every day	Smile
Being kind to others at break time	Thank you/star
Coming on time every morning for a week	Letter home/smile
Learning to do something new after trying hard	Certificate/sticker
Helping someone who was unhappy	"Well done"

Other suggestions the children made were: cross country run, badge, good work assembly, swimming, writing in your book, telling the class, going on a trip, taking a nice picture home.

Here is a list to stimulate ideas for encouragements, rewards, incentives, reinforcements you could use in your class.

Social

Verbal - when you use praise it should be convincing. Stereotyped "matter of fact" comments are of less value.

> *"That's right, you have... "*   *"That's good because...'*
> *"Thank you, I like that."*   *"That's really nice."*
> *"Great, that's smashing."*   *"You're really doing well."*

Telling the head teacher, another teacher, another child, school secretary, parents something good about the child in the child's hearing.

For variety and reinforcement ask questions about the achievement.

> *"Will you show me how to do it?"*
> *"How did you do that?"*
> *"That's wonderful, what did you use?"*

Non-verbal - physical contact should obviously be of an appropriate nature given the age of the child and should be consistent with school policy on touching.

Smiling

Expressions of amazement

Laughing

Nodding

Helping child with a task

"Thumbs up" sign

Standing near child

Expressions of delight

Clapping

Making eye contact with child

Playing games with child

Winking

Sitting near child

Putting child's work up on wall

Other

Comments on book

A "good note" to take to the head teacher or to take home

Positive comments about the child by classmates

Showing work to the class

Class celebration.

NOTE: Punishments may be rewards! What may look like a punishment for one child may be a great source of attention and reward for another child, such as being kept in at break time.

Activities

Giving out and collecting the books

Playing with toys and games

Free time

Seeing a film

Wearing a badge

Sitting in the teacher's chair

Watching television

Extra playtime

Playing the piano

Preparing for lessons

Cleaning the blackboard

Staying in at break time

First in the dinner queue

Being a class monitor

Helping a classmate

Listening to music

Delivering messages

Using a stopwatch

Being "in charge" of other children.

Extra time on the computer

Feeding the gerbils

Wearing perfume

Turning on the T.V.

Taking pet home for weekend

Playing with puppets

Extra P.E.

Writing on the blackboard

Closing the curtains.

Tidying up after lessons

Playing outside

Water the plant

Helping the caretaker

Choosing a song

Rewinding the video

Extra Craft or Art Work

Allowed into play area

Using a typewriter

Concrete

Those with little or no cost.

Equipment or materials pupils can "rent" for a night and take home
Stars (to be placed on a chart)
"Good" badges to wear
Smiling faces
Stars, transfers or stamps that may be exchanged for other things

Those with significant cost.

Small toys or games	Plasticine
Sweets (Smarties, Jelly Babies)	Drinks (squash, milk, etc.)
Colouring books	Comics
Puzzles	Dot-to-Dot pages

Special materials (e.g. coloured chalks or pencils, paper, felt tip pens).
Small snacks (crisps, raisins, apple piece etc.)

Mazes	Playing cards
Clay	Kites

Internal (self reward)

Try to emphasise the satisfaction of doing something for its own sake or because it is the "right" thing to do. Encourage the child to use positive self-talk and to value him or herself:

"Great, I've finished."   *"It was hard but I did it."*
"That was my idea."   *"That's all my own work."*
"We worked together well on this."   *"Yes! I can do it."*
"I gave it my best shot."   *"I thought I couldn't but I did."*

Activity - choosing appropriate rewards.

From the list above, and drawing on discussions with the pupil, classmates, parents or colleagues, select a range of possible rewards. Only time will tell which are the most effective and easiest to administer.

Child	Possible rewards (immediate and longer term)

D. Planned ignoring.

A vital part of the programme involves planned ignoring. This is a very difficult strategy to use effectively. Obviously you are not expected to ignore everything the pupil does. That would be impossible. It may even be dangerous. As teacher you have a responsibility to the pupil under concern and to the rest of the class. Some actions you cannot and must not ignore.

Ignoring must be used consistently, as the following quotation explains:

> *Many teachers who believe they are "ignoring" misbehaviour may, in fact, be inadvertently reinforcing the behaviour they wish to decrease, either by occasionally forgetting to ignore the response or by unwittingly attending to the behaviour, often non-verbally ... Being able to engage a teacher in a brief, perhaps even unpleasant, conversation or catching the teacher's eye [may be reinforcing].*

(O'Leary and O'Leary 1977 p.57).

A common anxiety of teachers, however, is the reaction of the other pupils if one child is ignored:

A teacher may be fairly successful in ignoring attention-seeking behaviour, but the rest of the class ... will provide reinforcement.

(Docking 1987 p.246).

Admittedly, this may occur. However, in many instances the class will be sympathetic to your strategy and will often agree to co-operate in ignoring very attention seeking behaviours. The pupil may not be part of a group and may even be pitied.

I couldn't say she's got a friend (see Debbie Dawson, quoted earlier).

There is little chance in these circumstances of unwittingly giving licence to a group of classmates to misbehave in imitation. Children will generally react in a responsible manner when the teacher obviously ignores, in a planned way one, often rather isolated, child's irritating behaviours. This is **not** 'sending to Coventry'. Children can readily appreciate the difference between ignoring behaviours which spoil their lesson and totally ignoring a classmate all day. Terry Downs age 10 mentioned earlier, for example, was very attention seeking in class; the other children were, however, very sympathetic towards both him and his teacher's approach to helping him *"They've made a very positive effort, some of them in class, to befriend him and keep him out of trouble"*.

Despite these hurdles, all teachers do try to ignore particular activities some of the time. The exercise below is aimed at sharpening up this skill so that it can be used to maximum effect. As the responsible adult you must make your own judgment on when to use it. A common consequence of ignoring is an increase in the problem behaviour initially.

Teachers usually report that the pupil's behaviour becomes worse before it gets better

(Montgomery 1989 p.93).

Activity - sharpening up ignoring.

Although an odd question at first sight, it is vital to ask: what should you be doing when you are ignoring? It is not at all easy to ignore effectively; the trick requires practice. The technique ideally involves a neutral stance:

♦ Minimal eye contact (the pupil is likely to be hyper-sensitive to even fleeting glances in his or her direction).
♦ Minimal speech (the more you say the more chance of becoming annoyed and ladling out attention).
♦ A relaxed body posture (to give the non-verbal signal of not being disturbed).
♦ A composed face (again to give the correct message).
♦ An even tone of voice (when tense, voices can rise in pitch and children pick up this extra signal very quickly).

Minute by minute, class teachers have to judge whether or not to respond to particular pieces of behaviour in class. This judgment can depend on the child, the class, the lesson plan, how the teacher feels, how serious the behaviour seems etc. There are some times, however, when staff do, in fact, try to ignore certain behaviours, i.e. teachers don't always react to every misbehaviour.

The following questions may help you to examine your approach to ignoring in more depth:

Questions about ignoring

a. Recall times when you successfully ignored some piece of irritating behaviour in class (e.g. a child who sniffed constantly). Make short notes.

b. Now recall times when you tried to ignore some other piece of behaviour but in the end you had to respond. Make short notes.

c. What were the differences between a and b ?

d. When would you consider ignoring a piece of behaviour to be

    ... appropriate?

    ... inappropriate?

e. Think about the effect on other children if you ignore certain misbehaviours. What problems can arise and can you see ways round them (e.g. by enlisting their support)?

f. Think about the effect of ignoring a piece of misbehaviour for a few days then finally responding to it. What problems would arise ? How could you avoid these ? (e.g. by deciding to ignore from the start only those behaviours you can consistently continue to ignore over a long period).

g. Ignoring really means giving no reaction. Imagine watching a video of yourself trying to ignore a child's very irritating behaviours. What clues do you think someone else could spot that would indicate that you were, in fact, showing a reaction, even though you were trying not to? (Think about your posture, tone of voice, facial expression, looking in the child's direction etc.)

E. Punishment.

It is perhaps an unfortunate fact of life that teachers (and probably all adults) from time to time feel moved to apply some form of sanctions/ punishments for behaviours they find intolerable. As with ignoring and praising, this is another skill which it is not always easy to apply effectively. In the case of the attention seeking child the danger is that the "punishment" becomes the very reward the pupil seeks - more attention (this is the "punishment paradox" mentioned earlier).

> *some children ... seek punishment, because it is at least one way of gaining attention; the punishment does nothing to alter their behaviour for the better*
> **(Laslett and Smith 1987 p.221).**

In this section I will not explore ethical issues around punishment or confusion over its definition or even the controversy about whether in the long run it is effective or not (see Blackham and Silberman 1975, O'Leary and O'Leary 1977, Saunders 1979, Maines and Robinson 1991). The aim here is simply to clarify whether particular chosen punishments are real punishments, that is whether they reduce undesired behaviours.

A useful starting point is to consider, where appropriate, trying to use "natural consequences" or "logical consequences" (Balson 1982), such as, "no kit = no football", rather than arbitrary punishment such as "no kit = miss breaktime."

> *It is not the intention of an authoritarian punitive teacher to impose values and standards on students and demand compliance but, rather, to allow the reality of the natural or social order to impress students with the desirability or otherwise of certain behaviours.*
> **(Balson 1982 p.124)**

In school this is not always possible. Robinson and Maines (1988) stress the advantages of making punishments positive e.g. focusing on reparation, not retribution, to maintain self esteem. In many cases the need for punishment can be "organised away" by setting and sticking to clear rules and routines (Galvin et al. 1990). The careful systems behind the seemingly effortless working of a primary class, for example, are a tribute to the teacher's depth of planning experience and ability to do ten jobs at once. Children feel safe and are less likely to disrupt when they know exactly where they stand (Greenhalgh 1996).

However, for the purposes of the current programme there is another vital aspect to punishment: it can be a reward. It is essential to ensure that, for instance, being kept in at break to clean out the paint pots or complete extra work (with no one else in the class at that time to steal the teacher's attention away) or being sent to the head teacher, are not actually unintentionally rewarding for the child who is desperate for any kind of attention.

Your school may have its own rules about discipline. Try, however, to begin each day with a "clean sheet", particularly important for the younger pupils. If you are using some kind of special points system you may want to consider and reject loss of points as a punishment. The attention seeking pupil will probably end the day with no points and masses of negative attention in the process. By the end of the week you may have nothing to praise and nothing to "write home about" except misbehaviour. Of course, this does not mean that normal sanctions and loss of privileges should not apply. Simply, make sure that any pupil you feel to be attention seeking receives your positive attention at a high rate during the day or you will be trapped back into giving attention at his or her demand, for misbehaviour.

Activity - looking at punishments.

a. Make a list of the whole range of "punishments" you have at your disposal, from frowning at or speaking to the pupil, through extra work and detention right up to exclusion.

b. For each one, attempt to assess, for the pupil in question, whether the "punishment" will bring with it unintended "rewards" (such as getting your undivided attention or becoming the centre of attention in class for a few moments). Select those with minimum spin offs.

c. Try to imagine viewing a video of yourself carrying out a recent punishment with an attention-seeking child. Did you say a great deal? Was your face red? Did you shout? Did your voice go up in pitch? Did you look tense? Try to assess the level of attention you gave. Remember that even very tiny non-verbal messages can be very powerful.

3. Follow up and trouble-shooting.

This is the final part of the approach. While in the middle of all this activity (and trying to teach thirty other children) it is often difficult to get an objective view of progress as classrooms are such busy, demanding places. It is vital, however, to try to arrange another observation session (either by using a colleague or by placing yourself mentally in "observer mode" for a time and forgetting about the programme). This is particularly important for the attention seeking pupil who can be so demanding as to seem to fill all the space available and to create a strong impression of incessant demands (recall Michael Platt's teacher's comment *"He blocks me from all the other children"*).

This programme is not offered as a cover up for poorly resourced schools and over-stressed teachers working in socially deprived areas. Nor is it a substitute for imaginative teaching, thorough preparation and a positive school ethos. However, even the most carefully thought-out strategies in the most privileged surroundings can run into problems. The ideas offered below should address some of the more common pitfalls.

a. General points.

♦ If you have not already done so, read part II. This gives many further examples of how other teachers have met many of the problems you are likely to be facing.

♦ If the situation does not seem to be progressing well, talk to your special needs co-ordinator. A host of snags can arise. For example, sometimes other pupils in class begin to resent what they see as your special treatment of a "naughty" child.

The other children felt that it was not really fair that he should be rewarded whilst he was behaving so badly.

(Merrett 1993 p.102).

♦ If this occurs try to involve them in the programme, for instance, by increasing rewards all round.

♦ Attention seeking may appear along with, or be confused with, dozens of other problems: language delay, learning difficulties, social skills deficits etc. Your programme may include several different facets.

♦ It may be, however, that joint work with parents is needed if your pupil is particularly attention seeking. This is where the school's psychologist may become involved.

b. The programme structure.

♦ Being too ambitious is a recipe for disaster. Often it is best to look for small gains gradually achieved. For instance, rather than eliminating shouting out it may be possible to reduce its frequency. The down side of this is that small degrees of progress might get overlooked.

♦ Inconsistency between staff is very common, between teachers, auxiliaries, dinner supervisors, secretaries. Even modest attempts at joint discussion of approaches can bring dividends.

♦ Misunderstandings are all too frequent. One teacher who had picked up the idea of extinction (meaning not reinforcing a behaviour until it disappears) said his approach to a very attention seeking child who was bottom pinching was *"tell her to stop every time she does it - to extinguish it"*. He could not understand why the bottom pinching increased. 'Time out' is another area of confusion. Basically this means the child is not allowed access to reinforcements for a while. The secret, however, is to focus on 'time in'. Unless a high rate of rewards is available during 'time in' i.e. during normal lesson time, 'time out' will not work.

c. Rewards.

Three common dangers are:

♦ No rewards are actually achieved. The standard is set too high or the child is expected to behave well until Friday.
♦ The rewards are ineffective. The child does not find them rewarding.
♦ The rewards are not related to the desired outcomes. As one special school for children with emotional and behaviour difficulties commented, *"We increased his rewards but they weren't really [tied] to his behaviour"*.

Relying on material rewards can lead very quickly to satiation. Social rewards are most effective and should be endlessly satisfying for the attention seeking child.

McNamara and Moreton (1995) also suggest encouraging pair work (taking turns talking and listening to each other) so that children can give each other extra attention.

> *Much attention seeking and disruptive behaviour occurs because the pupils feel that no one is taking any notice of them ... If they receive attention through a 'pairs talking and listening' activity on a regular basis their need to get attention by acting out is reduced (p.38).*

Matters can deteriorate after a period of success. Harrop (1983) for instance cites the case of Billy age 11. His teacher noticed a worsening of behaviour and work after about seven weeks. She felt that *"... perhaps she had slackened off in her social reinforcement, or ... her attention might have lost its effectiveness"* (p.106). She decided to be more specific in her praise and *" [refer] to the fact that Billy was being quiet, working well, and so on"* (ibid p.106).

d. Ignoring and punishing.

Ignoring can be an Achilles' heel both for the teacher and the rest of the class. Consistency and persistence are vital but tremendously difficult to achieve. It is possible to enlist the support of the class in a sensitive manner (see for example the case studies in part II).

The procedures around ignoring can themselves be a rich source of obstacles. Quentin Baker age 17 in a school for children with severe learning difficulties liked to bottom shuffle, amongst other annoying habits. His teacher said she tried *"putting him in the corner as soon as he shuffles"* in order to ignore him. Quentin maximised the fuss about being sent into the corner and shuffled all the more.

Punishments such as cleaning up or being sent to the head are often themselves a rich source of rewards for the attention-seeking child (recall for instance Dave Norris who enjoyed being kept in).

e. Lesson flow.

In addition to the strategies outlined above which are aimed specifically at one pupil, you may find it useful to consider your approach to the class as a whole. Many packs such as "Building a Better Behaved School" (Galvin et al 1990) can help in this area. One special area of interest which is not always adequately covered in published materials, however, concerns lesson flow.

Teachers are amazingly skilled at carrying out a dozen tasks at once, meeting constant, contradictory demands and yet maintaining a smooth flow of work and interactions throughout the lesson. From time to time, however, hiccups occur in areas which the busy teacher may never have stopped to consider, as teaching becomes so automatic after a while. Although no panacea, honest consideration of this issue may reveal many potential flash points and bottlenecks in your teaching style which interrupt the smooth flow of interactions in class. These can add to the problems of dealing with any single pupil. A list of the most common difficulties is given below.

Activity - points to consider in helping lesson flow.

Apart from good lesson preparation and clear rules and routines a number of points seem relevant to help the flow of the lesson. Listed below are fairly common pitfalls and some suggestions for tackling delicate interactions with children of various age ranges. Adapt them as necessary for your age group.

Think back over a particularly bad lesson (this can be excruciating!). Consider those instances where anything interrupted the smooth running of your teaching. Discount the unexpected interruptions such as the fire alarm going off or a visitor walking in; concentrate instead on those interactions directly under your control, the 'fine detail' of your responses. How many items on the following list can you identify and take steps to address?

Dingle Dangles *
> Teacher says, "Now get out your books" then turns round to talk to the little charmer kicking the table. The children are left "dangling". Disaster looms.

Flip-Flops *
> Watch out for, "Get out your books" (flip) "No, write this down first" (flop). Chaos awaits.

Double Talk
> Don't talk till all the children are listening. Don't talk if they are talking. Try to get their attention first by looking, waiting and pointing, not by speaking / shouting.

Walkie Talkie Chaos
> Don't give instructions as they are moving to their groups. Give them before they start moving.

The Pre-emptive Strike
> As soon as we mention moving to a different part of the room, some of the children will start to go. So pre-empt this by saying "stay in your place for now" before giving any instructions about moving. (Similarly for getting out equipment.)

Warning Bells
> To prepare children for the end of an activity (so they are mentally geared up to finishing and don't start to complain about not having enough time). Give a two minute countdown as a warning.
> N.B. Every change of activity is a potential disaster area!

Machine Gunners
> Any new piece of equipment given out to the group can be used as a "machine

gun" to cause chaos. All material in these circumstances is a potential hazard. Don't give it out until they need it and know exactly what to do with it.

The 'Is this a question?' Question

Just say, "Let's try it again" if you're going to try it again anyway. Don't ask, "Shall we try it again?" if you don't really want an answer. Many children don't realise no answer is really wanted. They may shout out anyway.

Short Talks

Bearing in mind the ability level of the children and the short attention span of the youngest, the shorter the instructions, the better.

Devil's Work

Children misbehave when they have nothing to do in class. We need settling down / filling in / bridging activities where appropriate.

The Quiet Word

If a child misbehaves and you shout at the child across the class, this;
> ... disturbs all the other children
> ... makes him/her the centre of attention.

So:
- Walk up quietly while you are still teaching.
- Stand behind him/her.
- If things don't settle, try a quiet word in his/her ear.

Sprinkle Star Dust

It sounds corny but it's true, the more positive comments you quietly sprinkle round the class, the more co-operative the children are.

The Walkabout

Research shows that the more requests for "order" a teacher gives and the louder the teacher's voice, the noisier the children are. It's hard to see which is the chicken and which the egg, but attempt to break the cycle by giving fewer comments to the whole class. Try walking round quietly telling groups what to do. It takes a little longer but it can be much more effective.

The Side-step
Praise the children who are quiet.

The Stare - particularly for older children
Practice getting attention by waiting with an eye-brow raised and a confident quizzical stare in the direction of the least attentive child. Nearby children will often then support you in telling that child to be quiet or to turn round.

<u>Divide and Rule</u>

Especially for the very difficult high school class containing children who arrive at different times from the far corners of the building.

Have ready-prepared, easy to do, "settling down" work to hand for the first few minutes of a lesson. Don't try to give instructions. Give out the work sheets or quietly point to material on the board written earlier (or on flip chart paper prepared the night before if you can't get into the room before the lesson). Most of the children will actually start to do it. Your problem is then reduced to dealing with a smaller number of pupils who are not co-operating.

*adapted from Kounin (1977)

Case Studies.

These examples have been chosen to illustrate the flexibility of the approach in very different settings. The "success" or otherwise of the work is of secondary concern here.

The first study, written at the end of a course which used an early draft of these materials, highlights the clear thinking of one primary school teacher working with a moderately attention seeking boy.

The second case arose from some relatively unplanned work in a residential school for secondary age children with emotional and behaviour problems. The host local authority had changed the nature of the school, apparently with little or no training to meet the needs of a much more demanding intake. A meeting, called one Friday afternoon when the children had been sent home early, to address the needs of a particular boy, turned into a hair-raising, in-service training session for the whole school. All the staff, teachers and care workers, were very upset. Luckily, their commitment was still at a high level at that point. They gradually took on board the idea that Sam's behaviour was attention seeking, even though this meant examining their own interactions when they already felt very stressed.

Ken Turnbull, the child in the final example, displayed many unusual behaviours, particularly with regard to his interpersonal skills and mannerisms. He had a very rare brain condition. This was not normally associated with autism; however, there were similarities. Although from consultation with a regional expert it seemed that children who were strongly autistic would not respond to our approach, it became clear through our discussions that Ken probably would because he loved attention and praise. The teacher was also keen to try and very dedicated.

Case Study 1 - an individual approach.

<u>George age 6. Left-handed. Very small for his age. In mainstream.</u>

Points to note:

♦ The teacher's detailed identification of behaviours both to increase and decrease.
♦ The way she drew useful information from George.
♦ How the whole class became involved in her approach.
♦ The effectiveness of increases in rewards all round.
♦ The very limited use of loss of points. She ensured that George still earned many rewards each day.

Records passed on from previous school:

Enjoys cooking, Lego and wooden bricks. Responds well to praise. Enjoys stories. Kicks, nips, punches. Not allowed reading book home because of damage. Spoils work / models of others. Poor concentration. Stealing. Father more approachable than mother. Works well next to teacher.

Background:

Father not in touch now. Has younger brother and sister. Mother has not come into school to collect confiscated items etc. Concentration poor in written work. Good when modelling, Lego, painting, computer. In support teacher's group for help with listening and concentration.
Poor handwriting. Doesn't know first twenty common words yet (has 15/20). Poor writing. Average of one line with very poor spelling and no spaces. For appropriate reward can be encouraged to do more.

Behaviours to reduce at first thought:

⇒ Fighting at playtime.
⇒ Reacting aggressively in class.
⇒ Snorting.
⇒ Picking nose putting in other children's dinner.
⇒ Unfairly telling on other children e.g. for accidental knock.

After further observation these items were added:

⇒ Getting out of seat.
⇒ Spoiling other's work.

⇒ Refusing to do jobs for teacher.

⇒ Collecting all equipment in front of him e.g. felt tips.

⇒ Going to other tables / watching other tables doing different work.

Behaviours to increase:

√ Smiling at teacher.

√ Talking to teacher about topic work.

√ Bringing in topic-related items.

√ Sitting in seat.

√ Being helpful - offering to do jobs.

√ Being truthful about initiating fights.

√ Voluntarily answers to teacher's questions.

Discussion with Child revealed:

Likes	Dislikes
Coming to school Lego Playdoh Junk modelling Painting Library Large apparatus Small apparatus Time to move	News / written work Number work Playtimes (when cold)
Interests	**Looks forward to**
Snakes and ladders Electricity Percy Main Park Army displays Wants to be a fireman	P.E.

His "ideal school" would have climbing and choosing activities all day.

Programme.

First Week.

1. Fighting at playtimes was George's most reported 'problem'.
   The school policy has been changed now as this problem is growing throughout the school. If a child fights he misses a PE lesson or swimming (older children). George immediately missed three PE lessons but hasn't lost any in the past few days. When he hits back in the playground it seems to be other children starting the trouble, not him. The rest of the class have confirmed this.

2. His most irritating habit was snorting and picking his nose. I tried to ignore this but was unable to. I decided to warn him to use a tissue and if he did it again I would knock two class points off without saying anything. He rarely picks his nose now and 'snorts' much less.

3. A number of children leave their seat unnecessarily when they should be working. I have started a system now and I write the child's name on the board if they leave their seats. Reward for those who don't. Everyone got a biscuit this week!

4. I am encouraging George to bring things of interest into school. All children receive class points for this now. Whenever George is behaving well I try to use him as a 'good example'. I now hand out spare milk to those who tidy up well after an activity. George responds well to this reward. George's attitude towards me and the other children has improved a good deal since I have been giving him a lot more attention. The other children seem to be 'on his side' more now instead of pointing out his poor behaviour.

One week later

George continues to lose PE lessons for fighting or insolence to dinner ladies, particularly lunch times. Little snorting now. Getting out of seat has reduced.

One year later

Does not snort. Does not pick his nose. Does not spoil others' work. Mainly stays on seat. Still occasional aggression at break and in class. Some tale telling and collecting equipment. Overall, settled and acceptable in class.

Case Study 2 - a whole school approach.

<u>Sam Harton, age 14, attending a residential school for children with emotional and behaviour difficulties.</u>

Points to note:

♦ How one child can appear to become the focus of a whole staff's attention.

♦ That even when most teachers seem to see little light, there are usually some positives to build on.

♦ Given an opportunity to focus on solutions and to share concerns, staff can address even seemingly intractable problems.

♦ A vital breakthrough occurs when a pattern is detected in apparently unrelated incidents.

♦ Starting with a list of unacceptable behaviours (which is fairly cathartic for most adults!) can actually be a powerful route to identifying positive targets. The negatives don't stay negative for long.

Sam's constant running away was causing a great deal of concern as, at age 14, he seemed to be "at risk". He had been known to the Educational Psychology Service for some time. He was a friendly, attractive "impish" boy to talk to. Although admittedly of below average ability, his reading and arithmetic levels were still many years below his age level. They had always been well behind what could reasonably have been expected from him.

When age 11, Sam had been placed at an Assessment Centre because of poor attendance and some criminal offences. This led to a placement at a more specialised Social Services Unit. Unfortunately he did not settle there and he was eventually placed at a residential school outside the area, for children with emotional and behaviour difficulties.

Great concern was expressed by the Head of the school and Sam's social worker about Sam's running away from the school. It was felt that he was at risk because of his absconding and the school had had little impact on this. Apparently the local police were also fed-up with him and when an Inspector had come to the school to "give him a good telling off" Sam had more or less laughed at him. There seemed to be no trigger to his running away and he was not being bullied. Apparently one of the attractions for his running off was that he could stay in the nearby village with some girls that he had met there.

In school, several of the staff had different views of Sam. For instance, with one of the care staff he would come and chat and be friendly and seemed "like a little boy lost". Others reported a whole range of misbehaviours, particularly in class.

He was reported to be very irritating by having a nervous laugh, making silly noises and fidgeting. He would also be very stubborn and never want to give up an activity once he started. He would swear, refuse to work, walk out of the class and misuse equipment and could also be a danger to himself and other children. He would rarely stay on his seat and when he did he would often slouch. He was easily distracted from his work and would argue with the teacher and deliberately annoy him by being noisy when he was supposed to be quiet. He would back away from fights with other children but would annoy them, particularly when staff were around.

When we discussed his running off it was clear that "he grinned all over his face" when he eventually came back to school. One of the staff said "he gets hyped up on the attention of being one of the boys running off". His social worker also felt that "he enjoyed the chase" and all the excitement of running off and calling in the police. Everybody at school seemed to have Sam in the forefront of their mind; he seemed to come into all conversations.

Despite a great deal of discussion, many of the staff were reluctant to accept that

Sam's running off could be seen as part of a larger set of problems which could all be tackled in a similar way.

Staff found it easy to draw up a list of all his unacceptable behaviours and, after discussion, agreed to turn these into a more positive form such as "being quiet in class" rather than "making silly noises", "co-operating with requests" rather than "refusing to work", "staying in the classroom" rather than "running out", "asking for help" rather than "just sitting doing nothing" etc.

Several of the staff found it difficult to think of positive things about Sam or even to list activities he might enjoy. In discussion, however, it proved possible to bring out a list of some of his positive points and things he liked to do which could form a basis of a set of rewards to use for him. Finally staff agreed that he liked swimming and the computer and doing some jobs for them. He seemed to like the approval of some members of staff although he would tend to hide the fact. He was interested in rally cars and would join in some group activities such as five-a-side. He would come and sit on the knee of some staff and liked a cuddle and particularly enjoyed being with one member of staff and really liked his dog.

It was agreed to try to handle his running away in as low-key a manner as possible and simply to take reasonable precautions to supervise him. (Staff admitted anyway that, no matter how vigilant they were, he could always slip off if he wanted to.) It was quite clear that although he caused the school a great deal of worry, he was in fact quite "street-wise" and he rarely went further than the local village and just stayed there long enough to annoy everybody, including the police.
The school were also concerned about other children running off with Sam. It was, therefore, agreed that as well as attempting to tie rewards to Sam's regular attendance, the other children would be offered a group reward (going out in the mini-bus or extra videos) for not running off with him.

Until that time the staff had not been used to looking at matters in such a way. They began slowly, however, to see that his running off was just another attention seeking ploy along with the large range of other behaviours which they had worried about. Previously these had been seen as just individual "misbehaviours".

Despite some fairly negative descriptions of Sam at the start, it was possible by "picking everyone's brains" to come up with a list of rewarding activities for Sam, some to be used on a daily basis and some to be for weekends. These were used to encourage him to show his more positive side. Naturally, counselling still continued along with the school's other supportive activities.

Sam, unfortunately, left school for a Social Services establishment with rather closer supervision, before the programme was fully worked through, despite encouraging early signs of success with the approach.

Case study 3 - a child in a day special school.

Ken Turnbull, age 7, attending a school for children with physical, sensory or medical impairments.

Points to note:

- The importance of not being distracted by the medical context of a problem.
- That many elements of the programme were already in place; the key, however, was to re-structure these.
- The aim of the programme was not to take up more teacher time but simply to re-direct existing efforts in a systematic way.
- That careful analysis is as important as commitment. A third party can often stand outside the issue and help change the perspective.
- The parental support.

Background.

Ken was born with a number of brain abnormalities. His parents were concerned about the development of rather ritualistic behaviours and also the slow development of his speech and social relationships. His perceptual motor skills, however, appeared to be developing well.

Following formal assessment Ken was provided with a Statement of Special Educational Needs and transferred to a school with a safe, protective, physical environment. He could express himself well in a simple conversation, although he had a large number of learned phrases. His response was not always appropriate or directly clearly at the listener. He could understand instructions with three key words and verb tenses, for instance "Who's climbed the ladder ?" Ken was quite active and had difficulty settling; his listening and attention skills were relatively poor. He tended to be fairly obsessive about certain things such as numbers, counting and ordering material but his main area of difficulty was in social interaction. He enjoyed adult company but had difficulties in relating to peers. At times he seemed to view other people as objects.

Recent concerns.

The class teacher was worried because "Ken's behaviour gets in the way of his learning". He had positive behaviours and could sit still, look, listen, be quiet and answer appropriately for short periods. He had improved since his inhaler had been suspended. She noted, however, a number of difficulties in relationships with peers.

The other children were discouraged by his behaviours and tended not to include him in play or group work. He would attempt to take over games and for instance pushed a child away, pulled a chair out from under or switched a machine off. In group play he might take toys from other children, loudly repeat sentences he knew or simply "be in the way". He would tend to reinforce dislike from others by, for instance, removing cushions from a chair-back and throwing them across the floor, snatching toys, food or cutlery, pouring his own drink into other children's beakers and obstructing the movement of wheelchairs. Aggressive behaviour towards others included tripping them up, blowing on them, twisting their fingers or kicking.

With one adult working with him 1:1 Ken could behave quite well but the teacher felt he used a range of tactics to ensure that he kept that contact - such as repeating everything very quickly; bobbing up and down saying "stop talking" when asked to do something; pulling the adult's arm away or their book; at times not looking or listening; or, for instance, rolling his head all over the adult's chest and pushing up hard when cuddled in. Ken was also seen to trip staff up when they were carrying objects and would at times refuse to come to work unless cajoled and given 1:1 attention.

Mrs. Norton, the class teacher, felt that Ken thought "being naughty was good fun and was more worthwhile than being praised for good work". He loved to act out characters from naughty stories and it was clear that he knew he should not hit, trip and annoy.

As well as these difficulties in class, Ken displayed a number of obsessional behaviours, for instance looking round for any numbers to distract himself with such as calendars or number lines or repeating large chunks of video dialogue. At times he would jump up and down, flap, bite his own hands, self stimulate and produce "John Cleese silly walks" after being told off in the yard.

Recent attempts to support Ken.

Mrs. Norton had tried a number of tactics in class such as giving him 1:1 attention as often as possible, sending him out for a few minutes to sit on the "sad chair", giving him praise for good behaviour and happy faces. She also told him clearly what was expected and he enjoyed treats and privileges. Occasionally he was sent off to another class to cool off.

Mrs. Norton summed his difficulties up as follows: "He wants one to one attention all the time". At a recent review his mother commented, "If you poke a child someone will come and tell you off. That's a way of getting attention".

At this point it was agreed to refer Ken to the Regional Child Psychiatry Unit for further assessment. In the meantime, while exploring what could be done in class

while we waited for this, the teacher agreed that she could view much of his behaviour as attention seeking. She happily began a programme along the lines outlined earlier.

The current programme

Mrs. Norton quickly agreed that Ken responded very well to praise. This was a powerful reward. She was very easily able to turn those behaviours she was concerned about into a list of 23 positive behaviours for which he could be commended. She called this Ken's "praise list".

The programme began to take effect quite quickly as Mrs. Norton began to seek out, and respond more to, these positive behaviours. After a couple of weeks she reported that Ken had improved all round, even in music where he had generally behaved very poorly. During this period his mother also supported the school by providing extra reinforcement at home.

Ken's praise list

When playing

1. For standing alongside or watching quietly
2. For passing a toy
3. For asking another child what they wanted
4. For touching or hugging gently
5. For fetching a chair for another child
6. For picking up a child's crutches and hanging them up
7. For moving out of the way of a wheelchair
8. For sitting in his own space
9. For leaving the wheelchairs alone
10. For giving out books and pencils

With all staff

1. For listening carefully
2. For listening quietly
3. For touching gently
4. For staying in his own chair space next to an adult
5. For coming to work when asked
6. For moving out of the way

In group work

1. For listening when asked
2. For watching another's turn
3. For waiting quietly for his turn
4. For being quiet

Lunch and Playtime

1. For walking along without touching others
2. For acting out "good" characters in plays
3. For leaving other's dinner or drink alone

Recording steps to Success

The following pages provide a variety of charts on which a pupil's progress towards an identified target can be recorded.

It is important to plan the programme in a way which ensures success, e.g. where there are a lot of steps, (the snake, page 65), the steps must be small enough for success to achieved within a short time span.

The last two charts, Staircase to Success and Overcoming Hurdles, allow for incremental targets to be written into the programme to build upon success over time.

The resources are freely copiable to the purchasers of the publication.

63

65

Staircase to Success

Overcoming Hurdles

Part II - The context.

Introduction - the child and the family.

> *The basic principle behind the development of many common behaviour prob-lems is that children work for attention from others ...whether it is positive ...or negative.*
>
> **(Webster-Stratton and Herbert 1994 p.240).**

Attention seeking children make some of the greatest demands teachers have to face in class. Montgomery (1989) reports this to be the highest priority of all behaviour problems identified by teachers on in-service courses (p.8). Ashman and Elkins (1990), Balson (1982), Grimshaw and Berridge (1994) and Peagam (1994) also em-phasise its high incidence. The description is regularly used in conversation in schools but written material is scattered about in the literature, with sometimes only fleeting mention and different terminology (*"attention getting"* McManus 1993; *"delinquent or nuisance attention seeking"* Stott 1980; *"attention getting mechanism"* Dreikurs et al 1971). This book aims to collect these ideas together into a coherent whole and provide practical advice for the class teacher who in many instances may be forced to respond, of necessity. To put the concept into its full context, however, it is helpful to consider initially some out of school aspects.

First, it is important to note that, although a source of much distress, attention seeking may not necessarily be a barrier to later success, as the following extract reveals:

> *By the time he was five, he had become exceedingly mischievous and had a passion for practical jokes...he began another practice - the telling of stories...real whoppers that often threw his mother and neighbours into an uproar ... he ran away frequently, often to go play near the dangerous and forbidden creek... He would have rated highly on ... attention seeking... as an adult Sam was almost invariably the center of attention ... and he is recorded as having openly sulked when he could not keep the stage ... he demanded constant attention and was annoyed when he failed to get it.*
>
> **(Sears 1961 p.11, 12, 30, writing about the life of Sam Clemens/Mark Twain)**

The term 'attention seeking' appears little in the relevant psychiatric literature. It does not, for instance, rate an index entry in Rutter et al's (1994) mammoth and highly regarded text on child and adolescent psychiatry and is not conspicuous in the body of the work (psychiatrists tend to conceptualise the issue rather differ-ently). Although many attention seeking children could be dealt with in a medical setting, it is likely that most are not. This book is aimed at those who do not receive such support.

Attention seeking in children could arise for a whole host of reasons: abuse, neglect, learning difficulties and so on. It is obviously vital that these conditions are recognised and, where possible, addressed. The programme described earlier is not meant to be a substitute for such action. Gray and Richer (1988) for example regard attention seeking as *"a classic form of anxiety-based behaviour"* (p.21). Their approach of raising the self-esteem of the pupil and examining management styles in class would not be inconsistent with many aspects of the approach outlined in part I despite the difference in analysis.

While attention seeking could be a result of emotional deprivation or rejection at home, in many cases parents are extremely involved with the children and often desperate for a better relationship. The difficulty seems to occur in otherwise quite "normal" families and is not related to class, educational background, age, gender, financial or marital status. A recent survey of referrals to an educational psychology service from two high school/ middle school/ first school pyramids over a period of three years, revealed rates of incidence of between 1.4 and 2.8 per thousand (between four and seven per high school pyramid per year) for areas of relatively high and relatively low socio-economic status respectively. These figures could, however, be heavily influenced by a number of factors such as limits on the number of referrals accepted and certain schools' responses to in-service training on the issue, and should thus be seen as a rough measure only.

The vast majority of referrals (86 %) were boys. Most research notes the high rate of referral of males (strangely, however, in the few published case studies of attention seeking pupils unearthed, girls figure quite prominently, see later). It is tempting to speculate that, amongst the scores of complicated influences on boys' behaviour, early parental approaches could be one component which sets the context for later attention seeking cycles. As Maier (1988) notes *"from the very beginning of infant care, parents' reactions to sons tend to be different from their reactions to daughters"* (p.139).

Apart from the cited sources, the children mentioned as case examples drawn from the present study were white. During the period considered, a handful of children from Chinese and Asian families were referred, but only for learning difficulties. I have no reason to suspect, however, that the approach would not be relevant to children from other ethnic or cultural backgrounds, indeed anecdotal evidence from colleagues confirms this. In addition, Peagam (1994) points to the high rate of attention seeking behaviour and exclusions amongst Afro-Caribbean children and thus opens up possibilities of another line of support here amongst a complex mixture of other factors.

One upsetting feature of attention seeking is the way in which the interplay may go unrecognised over many years. Billy Harvey had been in and out of a number of schools, homes and assessment centres when I met him. While he undoubtedly had a range of needs and had encountered caring staff, effective approaches to his behaviour had never been organised. An important element in the therapeutic system he required was thus absent.

> Seaton School - 1977: His teacher recorded, "Billy never responds immediately to any spoken request or comment, but will stand or move in the opposite direction until he obtains undivided attention ... he craves love and demonstrations of affection ... He is an extremely meddlesome child, he cannot pass an electric socket, light switch or tap without interfering with them. ... Billy does not speak, he shrieks ... he rarely sits still and listens to a story, he is constantly fidgeting and disturbing the other children."

> Armstrong House Assessment Centre - 1978: Billy was reported to tease and kick the other children in order to get them into trouble. He was also seen to cling onto adults and follow them about so that it became "claustrophobic" for the people involved. He was seen to enjoy an audience and to deliberately speak loudly to draw attention to himself. If not receiving individual attention he was lost for something to do.

Glebe Crescent Children's Home - 1981: He will insist on switching on washing machines and will play with power sockets, television sets and gas cookers, etc. He is very affectionate and does not like staff to leave him. He can, however, be moody and sulk easily and does not like to be checked.

Taylor High School - 1981: Billy was "excitable" and could not sit or stand still. He fidgeted and lacked concentration and disturbed the class by shouting and singing. He used a variety of tactics to avoid work, such as complaining the sun was in his eyes or that he needed a drink.

Carlisle House Assessment Centre - 1982: Close examination of many items on the Bristol Social Adjustment Guide showed a common thread: the many and varied ways Billy could gain attention, often through "misbehaviour." Examples of these were "shuts self in room or runs off when corrected; screams and has tantrums; tires people with constant chatter; is a nuisance if adult is occupied by another child; restless and fidgets, etc."

Craghall Dene Children's Home - 1982: A similar pattern continued in this although it should be pointed out that he was in fact one of the older children there (14 years) and was thus able to exert more influence. The Housemother reported that he was very active, that he would insist on playing with washing machines, ovens, etc., that he had tantrums and would run up and down outside the home threatening to run away, that he would "take on" staff if he or another child were chastised, and that he demanded one-to-one attention from staff even though there was only one member of staff on duty.

Some children whose problems develop in a very extreme way may also display attention seeking in school as part of their difficulties. It is not, however, the argument of this book that tackling attention seeking will solve all ills. But there exist many young people whose relationships and quality of life can be changed, sometimes dramatically, by addressing the issue of attention seeking directly. Part of the work needs to be done at home, and the benefits of parent training for a wide variety of behaviour difficulties is well established: *"Reviews of these parent training programs are highly promising"* (Webster-Stratton and Herbert 1994 p. 24). Unfortunately, as the authors point out, 30% to 50% of cases where intervention has focused on the home setting do not generalise to the classroom, so direct school based work is needed. Their survey admittedly concerned so called "oppositional-defiant" and "conduct disordered" children rather than those who crave attention, but the findings must raise some question marks about the efficacy of a parent-only focus without a simultaneous school involvement.

Teachers often express concern that behavioural approaches simply sweep the "real" problem under the carpet. In many circumstance, it is apparent that dealing with attention seeking is not simply "treating the symptoms" and "hiding the underlying problem" - instead, **the attention seeking has become the problem.** As Morgan (1984) explains,

> *...the bizarre behaviour **was** the problem; his 'disturbance' was no more nor no less than the bizarre behaviour, and was not some separate underlying entity that we should assume existed as well* (p.3 emphasis in original).

In very many instances, once more appropriate patterns of interaction are established, experience shows that the pupil may become indistinguishable from his or her peers; in other words, the attention seeking was indeed the problem.

It is to helping the school related difficulties of such children that this book is aimed. To flesh out some of the issues around attention seeking and provide additional ideas for the teacher running into difficulties with the programme outlined earlier, a short review of the background literature is provided.

Attention seeking - background literature.

Much of the theoretical work on attention seeking unfortunately does not emphasise educational settings. This literature is briefly discussed later with a focus on the school situation where possible. Potentially of more immediate relevance to the class teacher are case study examples. A selection of these is included for illustration. The shortcomings of published examples, however, is that they often gloss over classroom reality, and as teachers will readily confirm, the devil is in the detail. This is particularly relevant when we note that attention seeking children absorb so much of a teacher's time (according to Schwieso and Hastings 1987 they receive *"three times as much praise and twice as much criticism as the average pupil"* p.125).

(1) Case study examples.

Amongst other issues the following points may be noted in the case studies:

- The wide range of attention seeking behaviours displayed.
- The relative unpopularity of many of the children.
- Teachers' frustrations.
- The long standing nature of the difficulties in many instances.
- The generally good ability level of the children.
- Advantages of staff sharing ideas.
- The use of ignoring by both class mates and staff.
- Low key handling of anti-social behaviours and aggression.
- The lavish use of praise.
- The need to build on existing positive behaviours no matter how small.
- The length of the intervention and possibility of regression.
- Problems arising when trying to observe such a personal, interactional condition.
- Difficulties due to mis-application of behavioural approaches.
- The need not for more teacher attention but for re-directed teacher attention.

Maureen
Galloway (1976) describes Maureen, age 11, in her first term at comprehensive school:

> ... in lessons which she did not like she either ran out of class or called attention to herself in a variety of ingeniously disruptive ways ... running round the school barefoot ...frequent loud "accidental" burps ... exquisitely timed to have maximum disruptive effect... she was not really popular (p.50).

Maureen reinforces the idea that such children often do not form part of any friendship group in class, but may be pitied, isolated or despised. In this case, the teacher recognised her behaviour as attention seeking *"and was reluctant to gratify [it] ...by caning her"* (ibid p.51 - a reassuringly enlightened response from the days of corporal punishment). The example also emphasises the long standing and recalcitrant nature of the difficulties often faced by the class teacher :

> *By the time Maureen went to school she had been learning for five years that the way to make grown-ups take notice of you was to be naughty* (ibid p.52).

The desperate reaction of the adults is highlighted:

> *The succession of teachers tolerated Maureen and tried to find ways of interesting her, but when their patience was exhausted, they soon learned that a slap would calm her down, if only for a day or two* (ibid p.52).

A joint discussion of all staff revealed that she could perform well in certain subjects. She was quite an intelligent girl. She responded well to special attention such as being register monitor and in lessons where she had been a "particular nuisance", teachers *"agreed to find her some small but useful job to do, such as helping them clear up at the end of the lesson"* (p.53). The case study thus also underlines the power of sharing the issue with all relevant staff.

Elizabeth.

Wade and Moore (1984) outline the case of Elizabeth, age 10, whose difficulties began when she changed class. She was one of eight children and also a twin, but "slower" than her twin brother. At home she was *"moody, resentful and tantrummy"* (p.27). She was tremendously attention seeking in class, and again, unpopular:

> *"At school she was spiteful and aggressive towards other children. She would also run off from school or have tantrums... There had been instances of her urinating in various containers around the classroom"* (ibid p.27).

The first area of concern targeted was her tendency to have tantrums:

> *... shouting, swearing, kicking and so on. We decided to tackle these by ignoring them as long as there was no possibility of her hurting herself or other children, or of damaging school property* (ibid p.27).

Her reactions were often violent, but staff found ways of dealing with this:

> *She would often stay out at playtime so that a member of staff would go and get her. She could then provoke a situation. The first time one of us did this she threw a tantrum and attacked with a broom handle. After that, we preferred to wait to observe her (for her own safety) but be unseen. When she arrived [back*

in class] nothing was said ... she was welcomed and requested to get on with her work. The length of time waiting outside gradually diminished (ibid p.27).

Her stealing was tackled in a low key manner which avoided confrontation and consequent attention:

The successful method we devised was to say 'You haven't by chance seen Darren's rubber? I'd be grateful if you could help him find it'. Nearly every time the lost article was recovered. We never did completely cure Elizabeth of her pilfering but certainly stopped her from taking items home (ibid p.28).

Her spiteful and aggressive behaviour was treated in a systematic manner:

Instead of dealing with Elizabeth first by removing her from the scene and reprimanding her, all the initial attention and a great deal of sympathy were given to the victim. The other children in class also responded to the hurt child. During these proceedings, therefore, Elizabeth was totally ignored (ibid p.28).

However, ignoring was not the only strategy, praise was lavishly employed. Note how relatively minor existing positive behaviours were emphasised initially, as a vehicle for delivering attention:

While ignoring inappropriate but relatively harmless behaviour, we took pains to ensure Elizabeth's good behaviour was thoroughly praised and sometimes publicly rewarded... At first she was praised for almost everything she did correctly. Sitting on a chair or even picking up a pencil was noted with approval... As the days progressed praise was confined to specific acts of behaviour: being kind to other children; producing more than mediocre amounts of work; voluntarily tidying up (ibid p.28).

Gradually further rules were introduced:

... but as few [new rules] as possible. Work had to be completed. She should be polite to teachers (certainly no hitting or swearing) and she was not to be aggressive toward other children (ibid p.28).

As a result of the programme, her work improved "dramatically" and she was allowed, as a reward, *"five minutes on her favourite activity"* (ibid p.28).

In this example, the authors stress the lengthy nature of the intervention and how Elizabeth would often regress:

she would suddenly revert to some aspects of her previous behaviour ... [she was] obviously testing us... we reacted in the same way... even though we were taken by surprise because we had become less vigilant (ibid p.28).

They also emphasise the need for a calm and consistent response over the long term, even when the pupil's behaviour produces *"strong feelings such as anger and resentment"* (ibid p.29).

Stewart, Samantha, Mark and Jason.

Montgomery (1989) provides three case studies of attention seeking children. (Stewart, Samantha and Mark.) In addition, although not described explicitly as attention seeking, one other example, Jason, provides an interesting perspective.

Stewart age 9.

"Stewart was obvious from the first day. While other children were listening to a story, he was crawling from the front to the back of the class under the desks and through the children's legs" (ibid p.150). In addition food and pens and pencils "went missing" but turned up in Stewart's possession.

The teacher tackled Stewart's difficulties at a time when she had some support from a remedial teacher in class. She decided to *"ignore his behaviour if it was not disrupting or harming other children"* (ibid p.151). She also asked the other children to ignore him. She provided him with rewards *"I encouraged Stewart and liberally gave him team points if he was actually doing what he should have been. Reprimanding him loudly usually resulted in Stewart hitting the nearest child"* (ibid p.151).

Samantha age 9.

She had unpleasant habits such as *"licking her nose"* (ibid p.152). Samantha *"alienated herself from her peers. She delighted in making them feel sick"* (ibid p.152) As time went on, the attention seeking also became subtle, "cheating in her work" even though she was quite capable. Her behaviour then culminated in destroying her coat. The teacher used "catch them being good" amongst other approaches, to help Samantha.

Mark age 9 years 6 months.

"He is very much a loner and has no friends in the class or in the playground. He seeks affection and will talk to me quite openly in class, during playtime and at every possible opportunity" (ibid p.154). For his age, however, *"he appears to have a mature comprehension about what he reads, hears and sees and can explain himself fluently, although his manner is rather eccentric... he is capable of detailed, interesting stories"* (ibid p.154).

Mark displayed a range of behaviours which could bring him attention:

> *restlessness, touching other children, picking [his] nose, crawling under desks etc., dropping things thus providing excuses to grope around rocking on [his] chair, laughing quietly at nothing in particular, staring at his neighbour until*

their attention is obtained, moving furniture about, losing worksheets or destroying them, humming, banging under desk with feet (ibid p.154)

The teacher adopted the following approach:

Made rules explicit, ignored non-damaging behaviour, gave praise and attention when his behaviour was satisfactory, and reprimanded other children when they made a fuss about his behaviour (ibid p.154).

The ignoring was difficult so the teacher explained it to the class and asked them not to worry. He enlisted class support, and:

... made it quite plain that they often made things worse by fussing over nothing and were often quite willing to put the blame on Mark when he was not the only one at fault (ibid p.155).

In addition to this programme, the teacher arranged help for his spelling difficulties and provided extra work to stretch him. After a stable period he suddenly regressed towards Christmas, then began to settle in the new term.

Jason age 10 years 11 months.

Jason had had long absences from school and consequent difficulties in literacy. Assessment showed that he was not a very able boy. Observation revealed that he sat with his desk lid open, wandered about to chat to friends, scribbled, deliberately broke pencils and occasionally threw things. From the description given, much of Jason's behaviour could have been a result of his learning difficulties. To this extent he is not typical of the attention seeking children described in the rest of this book. The teacher's approach of ignoring his misbehaviour and giving him attention and helping with his work only when he was seated at his desk, however, proved effective. Both his work and behaviour improved.

Merrett (1993) describes three examples:

Robert, Kenneth and a third child unnamed.

Robert.
The previous teacher of Robert age 6 years *"complained of his attention-seeking behaviour"* (p.36). In his present class *"He was unable to remain in his seat during group work. As a result he was continually interfering with other children"* (ibid p.37). As a strategy the whole class were rewarded for staying in their seats.

Kenneth.
Kenneth, in infant school *"craved attention"* (ibid p.88). The teacher decided to focus

on his calling out behaviour. Careful observation revealed, however, that this was not as frequent as she imagined *"a fairly common occurrence in behavioural interventions"* (ibid p.89). She decided therefore to focus on his not dressing after P.E. *"he would stand in his underpants ... looking lost and helpless and waiting for the other children to help him out"* (ibid p.89).

The teacher made up *"a cardboard track with a moveable train ... and eight stations, each one representing an article of clothing"* (ibid p.89). Each time he put on an item of clothing, the train was moved. The intervention began to have an impact immediately but was discontinued when he went into hospital.

Unnamed Child.
An unnamed child sought attention by *"putting up his hand to ask unnecessary questions, bringing his book to show the teacher the neatness of his work, the correctness of his first sum and so on"* (ibid p.103). The teacher began to record this carefully but *"as soon as he attempted to count the behaviour it virtually disappeared"* (ibid p.103). The author claims this occurs because *"quite unwittingly, the observer begins to behave towards the child in a somewhat different way"* (ibid p.103). This example highlights the difficulty of observation of a phenomenon such as attention seeking which depends on interactions. Change in the activities of one party, however small, may lead to changes in the other's.

Problems returned after half-term in a different guise *"he began to display much more immature behaviour such as lying on his back with his legs in the air and banging his head on the desk"* (ibid p.104). The teacher responded to this with a programme of "praise and ignore" which had a quick impact, then maintained the settled behaviour with occasional praise during the following term.

Anne, David, Patricia and Karen.

Murgatroyd's (1980) collection includes four case studies of children displaying aspects of attention seeking behaviour: Anne, David, Patricia and Karen. Karen was handled with what appears to be a rather confused approach. Patricia's difficulties appeared to coincide with marital violence in the home. These two are not included here. Anne's case is explored later and David's below. It should become apparent that the present author's attitude is that management in several of these examples left much to be desired.

David.
David is described as disruptive and easily distracted, lacking in concentration and seeking to gain friendship by any means. He also soiled himself frequently. He was from a very deprived background and his ability level would place him within the range of children with moderate learning difficulties. The author notes that

> *David's inappropriate soiling was a learned behaviour in that it was rewarding to him. Every time he soiled himself he received the adult attention he desired and needed* (ibid p.47).

The teacher who was new and young was quite understandably disturbed by the unpleasantness of the problem, however, *"Apart from responding to David each time he soiled himself, her attitudes towards him were totally negative"* (ibid p.47).

To deal with this situation, *"The time spent by the teacher coping with the problem was reorganised so that her attention could be channelled appropriately"* (ibid p.48). She was encouraged to praise him when clean (an example of not providing extra teacher input but redirecting her existing efforts). The programme also included, however, the advice to *"respond by expressing anger, by telling him he was naughty and by leaving him to clean and change himself"* (ibid p.50) whenever he soiled. The reader would be advised to ignore this latter suggestion (see for instance Kelly 1996).

(2) Theoretical background.

Introduction.

A vital aspect to understanding the problems which can arise from such actions lies in the **interactions** which can accompany them. A possible model of how attention seeking develops in the home environment would be as follows (although we cannot say that all attention seeking develops from relationship difficulties at home).

The need for attention is held to be a drive common to all humans (Coopersmith 1967). Children are even prepared to risk *"active physical and psychological abuse"* to gain attention (Browne et al 1988 p.197). As a result of life experience some children develop a great need for extra attention from their parents. There can be many triggers for this; Montgomery (1989 p.39) lists:

- Family upsets and quarrelling.
- During family break up and divorce.
- During severe parental illness and hospitalisation.
- When a new baby is born.
- In families where there is a lack of affection and support.
- At puberty with mood swings.
- Under peer group rejection.
- When other children in the family are favoured.

Children discover very quickly, however, that simply getting on with quiet play does not bring much response from adults. They may find out quite early on in life that the way to attract attention is not to sit and play peacefully but to shout, throw, break toys, push the TV over, poke the cat, annoy the baby. These behaviours bring mum or dad in pretty quickly. Parents report that even three week old babies can "fake" crying when they want attention, Wolff (1969). It would not be appropriate to label them "attention seeking" at such an early age; this is simply a form of communication.

The parent's (often angry) response answers that demand for attention, not in the way the average adult would enjoy, but for the child hungry for attention, this response is food and drink. Any response is better than being ignored. The parent thus unwittingly reinforces the very behaviour which he or she finds so irritating, but gains a temporary respite. The child is encouraged to continue as some form of attention results although, in the end, because of its "negative" nature, the attention is not fulfilling and the child has to seek more. The vicious circle is thus neatly closed. Carr and Durand (1985 a) summarise the interaction as :

A child behaves in an obnoxious manner. An adult responds by providing positive reinforcement such as attention. The child stops the obnoxious behaviour. In this sequence the child's obnoxious behaviour is positively reinforced (by attention) and the adult's attending behaviour is ... reinforced (by the cessation of the child's obnoxious behaviour) (p.237).

During these interactions, the adult, perhaps believing in some "medical" cause of the problem, and under stress and used to the idea that "punishment" (e.g. shouting) will reduce behaviour, cannot readily see their part in the chain; that their angry response is exactly what the child is seeking.

Dawson (1985) identifies five causes for attention seeking which appears in school:

♦ Developmental delay or faulty training - the child who is very dependent .
♦ As part of hyperactive or inconsequential behaviour - *"the pupil is uninhibited in seeking attention from the teacher"* (p.2).
♦ Anxiety - particularly for new pupils.
♦ Rejection by parents.
♦ Rejection by peers.

While this is a very helpful analysis, the full picture appears rather more complex, for instance with regard to the parents' role as outlined earlier. However, whatever the trigger, the child in class has to compete for attention with thirty other children. The poor teacher, pulled in a dozen different directions at once by his or her class, is very vulnerable and cannot readily ignore the child's actions in case *"other children ... provide the attention the teacher denies"* (Robertson 1989 p.126). How to deal with similar problems in the day to day world of the busy classroom is the focus of the programme in part I. The literature, reviewed below, provides further insight into the management of this situation.

Academic literature.

Major sources.

The concept of attention seeking appears in both popular and academic writing. It achieves little prominence, however. A recent computer search of an international data base, for instance, threw up only six articles mentioning the term in their abstracts since 1981, surprising when this is one of the most irritating and time consuming of behaviour problems in school. Five major sources bring different perspectives to the topic:

(1) D.H. Stott (1966, 1974, 1975, 1980) writings on the "maladjusted child".
(2) Hargreaves et al's (1975) work on deviance in the classroom.

(3) The research of R. Sears (1957, 1965) into child development.

(4) Publications by Adlerian authors such as Balson (1982), Dreikurs (1971).

(5) Blackmore and Murgatroyd (1980).

Amongst the points these authors raise are four vital issues:

♦ The differences between attention seeking children and children who misbehave as part of a group activity (even though, superficially, the behaviours may appear similar).

♦ An emphasis on attention seeking not being a problem that lies simply "within the child" but a problem that arises through the interaction of the child and the adult (which empowers the adult to break the cycle).

♦ The roots of attention seeking in the home setting.

♦ The difficulties arising from approaches which encourage "catharsis" rather than structured management of behaviour and its consequences.

D. H. Stott

D.H. Stott has written extensively on the "maladjusted" child. His Bristol Social Adjustment Guide (Stott 1974) is a questionnaire often used by psychologists, although now somewhat dated. One category in this questionnaire refers to the "inconsequential child" within which attention seeking is a sub-group covering responses to seven items out of sixty three in the whole questionnaire. Stott cautions against *"concluding that parental failure is always at the root of ... attention-seeking"* (Stott 1966 p.159) and presents a partly physical model: *"he suffers from an impairment of the ability to inhibit his impulsiveness"* (Stott et al 1975 p.64).

This work obviously raises the question of the extent to which single factor models are appropriate in explaining the development of attention seeking. There may well be some cases where a single well defined "cause" can be identified. In most instances, however, the attention seeking appears to develop gradually over a period of years.

In a family we often find that only one child displays the "problem". Parents are sometimes confused by this and insist "we treated them all the same". While parents may have intended to treat their children equally, in practice each child's experience of the family is unique : the oldest has younger siblings, the youngest has older siblings; children enter the family at different stages of the parent's relationship and possibly at different stress levels within the home. These can lead to critical variations in experience; one child may be jealous of the new baby, another may be unable to emulate a successful older sister. Balson (1982,1989) explores these ideas at some length within the framework of Adlerian psychology. The interactional nature of the development of the attention seeking is further illustrated in the next section through consideration of work on deviance.

Hargreaves et al.

Hargreaves et al (1975) examine the development of deviance in the classroom, in particular how initial "deviant" acts are amplified by the response they receive, thus leading to "secondary deviance". Although the authors do not focus on attention seeking as such, their analysis has many parallels. They illustrate their work with a number of children. Fritz is one child who needs attention (in the view of two of his teachers); the description of his behaviour is strikingly similar to that of the children in the present study. His teachers see him as special, different to the other pupils:

> *He's different in many ways from the rest of his peers...He will interfere with someone else's activities. He'll either pinch them, push them, have a kick at their legs as he walks past... At the back of the class he can be making various noises... All kinds of minor disruptive behaviours that you can think of, Fritz has done them... all the little classroom annoyances* (ibid p 178).

However, for all the "deviant" children, whether special like Fritz or not, the reaction of the teacher is crucial. If he or she responds by *"avoidance of provocation"* (ibid p 247) then the act will *"from the pupils point of view appear to have failed in its objective. The pupil has a problem"* (ibid p 247). Resolution of this problem then leads to "secondary deviation" i.e. the situation where the child's behaviour and the teacher's become locked in an interaction:

1. *pupil commits (for whatever reason) a deviant act*
2. *teacher takes avoidance-of-provocation reaction*
3. *pupil experiences a problem as a result of being ignored*
4. *escalation of deviance to resolve that problem*
5. *renewed avoidance-of-provocation from the teacher*
6. *alternation of 4 and 5 until...*
7. *teacher makes overt social control reaction.*

(ibid p 248)

If we substitute a phrase such as "attention seeking act" for "deviant act" or "deviance", we have a fairly clear description of the development of attention seeking and resulting interactions in class.

Discussion of deviance often centres on the group nature of such activities. Many of the children in Hargreaves et al's study are quite explicit about their joint intention to annoy the teacher. They sound rather like the boys in Willis's 'Learning to Labour' (1977). The example which follows could be that of an attention seeking child:

the kid still marooned from his mates crawls along the backs of the chairs or behind a curtain down the side of the hall, kicking other kids, or trying to dismantle a chair with somebody on it as he passes (Willis 1977 p.12).

It is clear from the context, however, that his behaviour is part of regular sub-group conforming activities; he's "having a laff" with "the lads". Many attention seeking children, by contrast, appear isolated and friendless, perhaps more like Fritz earlier. Their actions are often a desperate attempt to gain individual attention unlike the boy above, obviously well provided with "mates" and playing to their rules.

For those interested in pursuing recent debates around interactional theories of deviance, Tierney (1996) provides a good starting point. Part of the debate hinges on the way in which interactionists are claimed to have ignored the importance of those initial actions which trigger the cycle. In our case, while the teacher certainly responds to attention seeking in class, it is clear that to understand the problem in school we need to address both the pupil's behaviour in class and its origins at home. This redirects our attention to the family setting and the work of Sears and colleagues and the Adlerians below.

Sears et al.
Sears takes a behavioural approach to the study of child development. The infant is seen as dependent on adults. Sears examined clusters of behaviour associated with this dependency. Only one achieved statistical significance - negative attention seeking: *"Getting attention by joking, teasing, disruptive aggressive activity"* (Sears et al, 1965 p.33). Attention seeking was held to arise when punishment for irritating behaviour went hand in hand with rewards :

> *The situation in which the mother sometimes loses her temper over the child's dependency and sometimes responds sweetly.... or in which she becomes irritated but nevertheless turns her attention to the child and gives him what he wants*

(Sears et al 1957 p.173).

Sears rejects a notion of linear causation *"We are sceptical that there is any single direction of cause-and-effect... The whole relationship could be circular"* (ibid p.175) and *"the mother's double response of giving the desired attention in the midst of irritation is made more probable and a vicious circle is established"* (ibid p.174).

Without wanting to blame parents (they feel guilty and stressed enough as it is when they come to family therapy sessions), it is important to track the beginnings of difficulties in class back to management problems at home and here, joint work with home and school is usually the most productive approach. Other publications will tackle this issue in depth but for now, some further insights into the home setting will be drawn from the work of Adlerian writers.

Alfred Adler.

Alfred Adler has received renewed interest in a recent biography (Hoffman 1994). This records the (largely unrecognised) influence that he had on later figures such as Carl Rogers, Rollo May and Abraham Maslow and the field of humanistic psychology generally.

Within Adler's (1924) "Individual Psychology" the key to understanding a particular behaviour is to see it within the context of that person's individual view of the world and their individual decisions on how to respond: *"The development of personality, of a life style, is based on the opinions which the child forms about himself and others and of the goals which he sets himself"* (Dreikurs et al 1971 p.5). These goals make the understanding of later behaviour clear:

> *he may overestimate the importance of winning his parents' approval; he may find difficulty in accepting criticism; he may be overly sensitive and let others make decisions for him... he may try to control and manipulate... Some children may think that being good is the only way to have status* (ibid p.5).

For Adlerians, a strong motivation for all humans is to belong *"As a social being, each child wants to belong. His behaviour indicates the ways and means by which he tries to be significant"* (ibid p. 12). Thus, for instance, at the birth of a sibling who absorbs much parental time, a child may resort to any behaviour to attract the parent's attention back again and reinforce that sense of belonging otherwise *"he would be lost and worthless"* (ibid p.17).

> *The first child... may become discouraged upon the birth of the second child... He had been an only child for a period and has therefore been the centre of interest. He may believe that he has to be first... As a dethroned child with the birth of the second child, he may feel unloved and neglected. At first he usually strives... to regain his mother's attention by positive deeds. When this fails he ... may become obnoxious* (ibid p.47).

In school, four varieties of attention seeking are identified by Dreikurs (ibid p.16):

    (a) the active-constructive: "teacher's pet"
    (b) the passive-constructive: being "cute", children admired for what they are rather than what they do
    (c) the active-destructive: the "nuisance"
    (d) the passive-destructive : the shy, timid, dependent child.

The children of most concern in class tend to display type (c) behaviours - those we normally label attention seeking. The approach to handling these, described, for instance, by Dreikurs and colleagues and Balson (1982, 1989) is very close to that adopted in Part I.

Blackmore and Murgatroyd.

In exploring the case study of Anne, Blackmore and Murgatroyd (1980) propose that attention seeking arises through,

    (i) a delay in the *"separation-individuation"* phase of development of the child, with the teacher becoming substitute for the mother (p.37)

    (ii) *"an inability to achieve ... desired levels of arousal"* (p.38).

Anne is markedly physically aggressive and abusive and thus perhaps untypical of attention seeking children. The school adopt what seems to be a confused behavioural approach with limited success:

> *Whenever her work state enabled her to produce work, Anne was rewarded for doing so. Whenever her disruptive behaviour results in the teacher being able to be supportive.... the teacher is supportive* (ibid p.39).

The "support", however, appears to refer to the following sequence:

> *She always engineers a situation whereby I intervene and she is quarrelling with me. She will do her best (I feel) to get me to hit her. Once I have hit her she will usually then burst into tears. Then she'll sit on my lap quite happily (which of itself is strange, since normally she won't let you touch her) and let you cuddle her whilst she cries. Then she really talks. It's a catharsis really. When we've had this reconciliation she then wants to please. She'll say she loves me .. [then] works like a mad thing* (ibid p.28).

Those who wish to pursue this approach may be advised to reconsider, this "catharsis" could be part of the reward the child seeks (a "reinforcement trap"). As Patterson (1982) points out:

> *If the child "won" by using a temper tantrum, then he will not only feel better but he will be more likely to do it again. The catharsis theorists accurately portray the fact that the child feels better after a tantrum, but these theorists ignore the reinforcement trap* (p.147).

Minor sources.

In addition to the main sources already discussed , a collection of other references to attention seeking is outlined below:

Only a small number of articles refer explicitly in their abstracts to any form of attention seeking or, in particular, to attention seeking in children. Peretti et al (1984 a and b) focus on the effects of parental rejection on attention seeking. Taylor et al (1993) explore the different contexts which could lead to attention seeking with one adolescent (e.g. setting events, presence or absence of peers and familiar adults etc.). Taylor and Carr (1992) provide a comparison of attention seeking and socially avoidant children in a special school setting. Their analysis rather simplistically concludes that:

> *adults respond to problem behaviours that occur under conditions of low adult attention by increasing attention. This response, in turn, terminates child problem behaviours* (p.331).

It would be nice if life were that simple!

Carr and Durand (1985 b) claim, in considering children with learning difficulties, that *"the factors responsible for the maintenance of behaviour problems fall into two broad classes: escape behaviour … and attention-seeking behaviour"* (p.112).

Several academic texts in relevant areas such as education, child development, behaviour difficulties or psychology mention attention seeking within the body of the material but rarely list it as an index entry. A selection of case studies uncovered in these sources was provided earlier.

As mentioned previously, authoritative works in child and adolescent psychiatry such as Rutter et al (1994) seem not to use the term at all. It is possible that a label such as "attention deficit hyperactivity disorder" could be much more readily applied to the children in some regions as rates of diagnosis of ADHD vary tremendously (Taylor 1994). Attention seeking, however, appears in some respects more akin to the "relationship disorders" described by Zeanah et al (1997) which are situated within *"a less well-accepted paradigm that defines disorders **between** rather than **within** individuals"* (p.86 emphasis in original). This model holds that *"most psychopathology in the first three years of life grows out of … disturbances in the primary caregiving relationship"* (p.87). One of the case studies demonstrating this approach interestingly illustrates a child who *"frequently interrupted and demanded his mother's attention"* (Sameroff and Ende 1989 p.140), although the diagnosis in this instance focused on inappropriate regulation of behaviour and mother's personality difficulties rather than attention seeking.

A wide range of behaviours in mainstream school has been associated with attention seeking in addition to those described in case studies earlier, such as: coming in late; convulsions; reading failure (Balson 1982). Feeding difficulties (nursery age) (Calam and Franchi 1987). Tapping pencils; whining; remaining in the corridor; wearing long earrings; stealing; lying (Dreikurs et al 1971). Shouting out; asking questions unrelated to work (Gray and Richer 1988). Teasing; exhibitionism; practical joking (Maier 1988). Tantrums; coming without equipment (Montgomery 1989). Repeatedly asking for work to be checked, fake illnesses (Pollard 1985). Scapegoating (Saunders 1979).

Obviously convulsions, feeding difficulties and illnesses, indeed any of the behaviours mentioned above or below, should not be routinely interpreted as attention seeking!

For children with learning difficulties attention seeking has been associated with:
- challenging behaviour (Harris et al 1996)
- self injurious behaviour of many varieties (Murphy and Wilson 1985)
- aggression; disruption; self stimulation (Taylor and Carr 1992)
- screaming, whining and crying; biting hands or hitting head with hand; saying "No" to adult requests (Carr and Durand 1985).

Conclusions from the literature survey.

Published material provides support for harnessing attention seeking as a valid and useful concept in exploring children's behaviour difficulties. However, more work needs to be done in:

- distinguishing it from other conditions (see discussion in part I)
- clarifying its definition and incidence
- establishing predisposing, precipitating and maintaining factors at home and at school.

Evidence from family interviews suggests that a number of influences may act as predisposing factors. A child may have had an accident, illness or handicap or may have been born at a time of marital difficulty or may have been adopted, for instance. In these circumstances, some parents expect unusual behaviour, or want to "make up" for past hurts. They often then report that they employed different (more lax) approaches to management from the earliest days, thus with the best of intentions, creating the very conditions to evoke unusual behaviours and forgetting the healing power of normal routine. In addition, simply being a boy seems to alter approaches at home. Parental disagreement over handling (one parent strict, one lenient) is frequently apparent. Other socio-cultural aspects may also be relevant.

Precipitating factors appear very varied and not always clear. Sometimes the attention seeking cycle seems to have no simple starting point. At other times a clear trigger is evident such as the birth of a sibling or change of school or going into hospital. Whatever the trigger, the response of the adult is then crucial. A misunderstanding of the nature of the problem can lead to responses which, despite the parents' best intentions, serve to lock the family into a very stressful spiral. There then seems to be a link between patterns acquired at home and behaviour displayed in class. Much more research is needed in all these areas.

Attention seeking - some cautions.

While being aware that even quite bizarre behaviour could be part of an attention seeking pattern, we should also be alive to the possibility that it may not be. A particularly poignant example arose in a Channel 4 documentary "Tales of Battered Britain" (October 18 1996) when one woman who had been sexually abused throughout her childhood and had on many occasions cut and mutilated herself explained *"It wasn't attention seeking or trying to commit suicide - it was a way of coping ... [I cut] to let the tension out"*.

Finally, it is vital while using the idea of "attention seeking" as a key towards developing effective support, not to lose sight of the child and his or her unique personality and strengths as Zarkowska and Clements (1992) aptly describe:

> *Too often people are 'labelled' only in terms of their problems. Thus a person who bangs his head ... becomes known as a 'self-injurer'. In fact, he may spend very little time banging his head but it tends to be very noticeable when it occurs ... the use of such a label prevents people seeing the whole person* (p.23).

Attention seeking - the lessons to learn.

We all need attention. Some children, however, crave attention to an extreme degree. What we call this situation, attention seeking or attention needing, is perhaps less important than the need to recognise it. Many teachers are genuinely upset by children who, despite their best efforts, appear to respond in a paradoxical manner. The frustration this causes is repeated time and time again, over many years in some instances. Those closest to the problem, often under considerable stress, fail to see the pattern. The most caring adult is the most vulnerable - those who have little interest in the child are not prey to these interactions. Perhaps, however, they engender other problems.

Western philosophy has been heavily influenced by notions of linear causation (Dell 1980). Circular causation is much more difficult to grasp, particularly when we are part of the circle. While we seek a "cause" or try to figure out the deep seated reason behind some unusual behaviour, while we think in terms of a problem "within" the child, we overlook the dance we have become unwitting partners in (Keeney and Sprenkle 1982). This book is tribute to that multitude of teachers (and parents) who have been able, without feeling criticised, to see their part in the cycle and lead the child out of the dance.

Bibliography

Adler, A. (1924)
The Practice and Theory of Individual Psychology. (trans. P.Radin).
London: Kegan Paul, Trench, Trubner and Co. Ltd.

Ashman, A. and Elkins, J. (1990)
Educating Children with Special Needs. London: Prentice Hall.

Balson, M. (1982)
Understanding Classroom Behaviour. Hawthorn: The Australian Council for Educational
Research Ltd.

Balson, M. (1987)
Becoming a better parent. London: Hodder and Stoughton.

Bandura, A. (1969)
Principles of Behaviour Modification. New York : Holt, Rinehart and Winston.

Besag, V. (1989)
Bullies and Victims in Schools. Milton Keynes: Open University Press.

Blackham, G.J and Silberman, A. (1975)
Modification of Child and Adolescent behaviour (2nd Edn). Belmont, California: Belmont
Publishing Company Inc.

Blackmore, M. and Murgatroyd, S. (1980)
Anne: The disruptive infant. In: Murgatroyd, S. (1980) Helping the Troubled Child: Inter
professional Case Studies. London: Harper and Row Ltd.

Blagg, N. (1987)
School Phobia and its Treatment. London: Croom Helm.

B.P.S. (1995) Attention Deficit Hyperactivity Disorder (ADHD): A Psychological Response to
an Evolving Concept. Leicester: British Psychological Society.

Browne, K., Davies, C. and Stratton, P. (1988)
Early Prediction and Prevention of Child Abuse. Chichester: John Wiley and Sons.

Calam, R. and Franchi, C. (1987)
Child Abuse and its Consequences. Cambridge: Cambridge University Press.

Carr, E.G. and Durand, V. M. (1985 a)
The Social - Communicative Basis of Severe Behaviour Problems in Children. In : Reiss, S. &
Bootzin, R.R. (Eds) Theoretical Issues in Behaviour Therapy. London: Academic Press, Inc.

Carr, E.G. and Durand, V.M. (1985 b)
Reducing behaviour Problems Through Functional Communication Training. Journal of
Applied Behavior Analysis, 18(2), 111-126.

Coopersmith, S. (1967)
Antecedents of Self -Esteem. San Francisco: W.H. Freeman and Co.

Dawson, R.L. (1985)
The Macmillan Teacher Information Pack (TIPS) : Attention Seeking. London: Macmillan Educational Ltd.

D. E S. (1989) Discipline in Schools. Report of the Committee of Enquiry chaired by Lord Elton. London: H.M.S.O.

Dell, P.F. (1980)
Researching the Family. Theories of Schizophrenia: An Exercise in Epistemological Confusion. Family Process, 19(4), 321-335.

Docking, J.W. (1987)
The effects and effectiveness of punishment in schools. In: Cohen, L and Cohen, A (Eds) Disruptive Behaviour: A Source book for Teachers. London: Harper and Row, Publishers.

Docking, J. W. (1993)
The management of behaviour in primary schools. In: Varma, V.P. (Ed) Management of Behaviour in Schools. London: Longman Group UK Limited.

Dreikurs, R., Grunwald, B. and Pepper, F. (1971)
Maintaining Sanity in the Classroom: illustrated teaching techniques. London: Harper & Row Publishers.

Galloway, D. (1976)
Case Studies in Classroom Management. Harlow: Longman Group Limited.

Galvin, P., Mercer, S. and Costa, P. (1990)
Building a Better Behaved School. London: Longman.

Gray, J and Richer, J. (1988)
Classroom Reponses to Disruptive Behaviour. London: Macmillan Education Ltd.

Green, C. and Chee, K. (1995)
Understanding Attention Deficit Disorder. London: Vermilion.

Greenhalgh, P. (1996)
Behaviour: Roles, responsibilities and referrals in the shadow of the Code of Practice. Support for Learning, 11(1), 17-24.

Grimshaw, R. and Berridge, D. (1994)
Educating Disruptive Children - placement and progress in residential special schools for children with emotional and behavioural difficulties. London: National Children's Bureau.

Grunsell, R. (1985)
Finding Answers to Disruption. London: Longmans.

Hargreaves, D.H., Hester, S.K. and Mellor, F.J. (1975)
Deviance in classrooms. London: Routledge and Kegan Paul Ltd.

Harris, J., Cook, M. and Upton, G. (1996)
A Whole School Approach to Assessment and Intervention. Kidderminster, Worcs: B.I.L.D. Publications.

Harrop, A. (1983)
Behaviour Modification in the Classroom. London: Hodder and Stoughton.

Herbert, M. (1981)
Behavioural Treatments of Problem Children: A practice manual. London: Academic Press.

Hoffmann, E. (1994)
The Drive for Self. New York: Addison Wesley Publishing Co.

Keeney, B.P. and Sprenkle, D.H. (1982)
Ecosystemic Epistemology: Critical Implications for the Aesthetics and Pragmatics of Family Therapy. Family Process, 21(1), 1-19.

Kelly, C. (1996)
Chronic Constipation and Soiling in Children: A Review of the Psychological and Family Literature. Child Psychology and Psychiatry Review, 1(2), 59-66.

Kounin, J.S. (1977)
Discipline and Group Management in Classrooms. New York: Robert E. Krieger.

Laslett, R. and Smith, C. (1987)
Confrontation in the classroom: children with problems and Confrontation in the classroom: teacher strategies. In : Cohen, L and Cohen, A (Eds) Disruptive Behaviour: A Source book for Teachers. London: Harper and Row.

Maier, H. W. (1988)
Three Theories of Child Development. London: University Press of America Inc.

Maines, B. and Robinson, G. (1991)
Punishment, the Milder the Better. Bristol, Lucky Duck Publishing.

McManus, M. (1995)
Troublesome Behaviour in the Classroom : Meeting individual needs. London: Routledge. (2nd Edn).

McManus, M. (1993)
Discipline in pupils excluded from schools. In : Varma, V.P. (Ed) Management of Behaviour in Schools. London: Longman Group U.K. Limited.

McNamara, S. and Moreton, G. (1995)
Changing Behaviour: Teaching Children with Emotional and Behavioural Difficulties in Primary and Secondary Classrooms. London: David Fulton Publishers.

Merrett, F (1993)
Encouragement Works Best: Positive Approaches to Classroom Management. London: David Fulton Publishers.

Montgomery, D (1989)
Managing Behaviour Problems. London: Hodder and Stoughton.

Morgan, R (1984)
Behavioural Treatments with Children. London: William Heinemann Medical Books Ltd.

Murgatroyd, S. (1980)
Helping the Troubled Child: Inter professional Case Studies. London: Harper and Row Ltd.

Murphy, G. and Wilson, B. (1985)
Self Injurious Behaviour. Kidderminster, Worcs: BIMH publications.

Patterson, G. R. (1982)
A Social Learning Approach. Vol 3: Coercive Family Process. Eugene, Oregon: Castalia Publishing Company.

Peagam, E. (1994)
Special needs or educational apartheid? The emotional and behavioural difficulties of Afro-Caribbean children. Support for Learning, 9(1), 33-38.

O'Brien, T (1996)
Challenging Behaviour: Challenging an Intervention. Support for Learning. 11(4), 162-164.

O'Leary, K.D. and O'Leary, S.G. (1977)
Classroom Management: the successful use of behaviour modification . Oxford: Pergamom Press Inc. (2nd Edn).

Peretti, P.O., Clark, D. and Johnson, P. (1984 a)
Parental Rejection as a Criterion Measure of Negative Attention-seeking. Psychologia, 27(1), 50-55.

Peretti, P.O., Clark, D. and Johnson, P. (1984 b)
Effect of Parental Rejection on Negative Attention-seeking Classroom Behaviours. Education, 104(3), 313-317.

Pollard, A. (1985)
The Social World of the Primary School. London: Cassell Educational Ltd.

Robertson, J. (1989)
Effective Classroom Control (2nd Edn). London: Hodder and Stoughton.

Robinson, G. and Maines, B. (1988)
A Bag of Tricks. Bristol: Lucky Duck Publishing.

Robinson, G. and Maines, B. (1994)
If it Makes My Life Easier to Write a Policy on Bullying. Bristol: Lucky Duck Publishing.

Robinson, G. and Maines, B. (1995)
Celebrations. Bristol: Lucky Duck Publishing.

Rutter, M., Taylor, E. and Hersov, L. (1994)
Child and Adolescent Psychiatry (3rd Edition). London: Blackwell Scientific Publications.

Sameroff, A.J. and Emde, R.N. (1989)
Relationship Disturbances in Early Childhood : A Developmental Approach. New York : Basic Books.

Saunders, M. (1979)
Class Control and Behaviour Problems. Maidenhead, Berks : McGraw-Hill Book Company Ltd.

Schwieso, J and Hastings, N. (1987)
Teachers' Use of Approval. In: Hastings, N. and Schwieso, J. (Eds) New Directions in Educational Psychology 2: Behaviour and Motivation in the Classroom. London: The Falmer Press.

Sears, R.R. (1961)
Mark Twain's Dependency and Despair. Paper presented to the Conference of the American Psychological Association, New York, September 1961.

Sears, R.R., Maccoby, E.E. and Levin, H. (1957)
Patterns of Child Rearing. London: Harper & Row Publishers.

Sears, R.R., Rau, L. and Alpert, R. (1965)
Identification and Child Rearing. Stanford: Stanford University Press.

Stott, D.H. (1966)
Studies of Troublesome Children. London: Tavistock Publications.

Stott, D.H. (1974)
Bristol Social Adjustment Guides (5th Edn.). London: Hodder and Stoughton.

Stott, D.H. (1980)
Delinquency and Human Nature. London: Hodder & Stoughton.

Stott, D.H. , Marston, N.C. and Neill S.J. (1975)
Taxonomy of Behaviour Disturbance. London: University of London Press Ltd.

Taylor, E. (1994)
Syndromes of Attention Deficit and Overactivity. In: Rutter, M., Taylor, E. and Hersov, L. (1994) Child and Adolescent Psychiatry (3rd Edition). London: Blackwell Scientific Publications.

Taylor, J.C. and Carr, E.G. (1992)
Severe Problem Behaviours Related to Social-interaction. 1. Attention-seeking and Social Guidance. Behaviour modification, 16(3), 305-335.

Taylor, J.C., Sisson, L.A., McKelvey, J.L. and Trefelner, M.F. (1993)
Situation Specificity in Attention-seeking Problem Behaviour - a case study. Behaviour Modification, 17(4), 474-497.

Tierney, J (1996)
Criminology: Theory and Context. London: Prentice Hall/ Harvester Wheatsheaf.

Wade, B. and Moore, M. (1984)
Coping with Disruption at School. Special Education: Forward Trends. 11(3), 27-30.

Webster - Stratton, C. and Herbert, M. (1994)
Troubled Families - Problem Children. Chicheser: John Wiley and Sons.

Willis, P.E. (1977)
Learning to Labour : How working class kids get working class jobs. Farnborough: Saxon House.

Wolff, P.H. (1969)
The natural history of crying and other vocalisations in early infancy. In: Foss B.M. (Ed) Determinants of Infant Behaviour, vol 4. London: Methuen.

Zarkowska, E. and Clements, J. (1992)
Problem Behaviour in People with Severe Learning Disabilities. London: Chapman and Hall.

Zeanah, C.H., Boris, N.W. and Scheeringa, M.S. (1997)
Psychopathology in Infancy. Journal of Child Psychology and Psychiatry, 38(1), 81-99.